CW00735787

·ITALY·
A COUNTRY REVEALED

DIVINAR
RER

Written by Adele Evans and Robert Hendrie Wilson
Senior Editor: Donna Wood
Senior Designer: Alison Fenton
Proofreader: Polly Boyd
Picture Researcher: Alice Earle
Image retouching and internal repro: Sarah Montgomery
Production: Lyn Kirby

Produced by AA Publishing

ISBN: 978-0-7495-5717-1 and 978-0-7495-5915-1

Published by AA Publishing (a trading name of Automobile Association Developments Limited, whose registered office is Fanum House, Basing View, Basingstoke, Hampshire RG21 4EA; registered number 1878835).

A03579

Colour separation by MRM Graphics Ltd, Winslow, Buckinghamshire
Printed in China by C & C Offset Printing Co., Ltd

The AA's website address is www.theAA.com/travel

Page 1: *Entrance to the inner court of Florence's Uffizi Gallery*
Pages 2–3: *A bird's eye view of St Peter's Square from the cathedral, Rome*
Pages 4–5: *Detail from the ceiling 'Dispute of the Blessed Sacraments' (1508–11), Raphael Room, Vatican Museums*

Contents

CAELORVM
TV ES PETRVS ET SVPER HANC PETRA
S·PETRI GLORIAE SIXTVS·PP·V·A·M·D·XC·PONTIF·V

Rome

Rome's fabled eternity is something of a paradox. It is both the most hallowed of holies in Christendom and the bloody backcloth to the most appalling evils of all time. Nevertheless, the great metropolitan community, located in central-western Italy where the rivers Aniene and Tiber converge, has been an inspiration for the world's greatest artists, writers, thinkers and scholars; its vices and virtues have been painted, penned and pored over for centuries; its very name is a byword for patience and tolerance in homilies about its not being built in a day and about how we behave 'when in Rome'. And for all its familiar infamy and glories, the beauty, grandeur and monumental richness of Rome's past consistently conspire to hypnotize the visitor.

According to legend, the city was founded by Romulus and Remus, the twins suckled by a wolf, on 21 April 753 BC. The archaeological evidence isn't so precise but it pinpoints the fusion of several rural settlements around the Palatine Hills into a city in the 8th century BC. This is what grew into the Rome of today: the Colosseum, relics of ancient government, the Forum, the House of the Vestal Virgins, museums, galleries and, of course, the fountains. Rome has about 4,000 of them, more than any city in the world.

With 10,000 visitors a day, the Vatican is Rome's big draw. For pilgrims, St Peter's Basilica is the holiest Christian site in the world, marking — in Christ's words to St Peter in 6ft (1.8m) high letters on the interior base of its dome — 'upon this rock I will build my Church'.

The interior of the magnificent 448ft (136.5m) dome of St Peter's was designed by the great Michelangelo but was not completed in his lifetime

Ancient Rome & the Colosseum

The ancient heart of Rome is dominated by the spectacular Colosseum, which is among the city's most visited tourist attractions. The site remains in good shape, by comparison with its neighbouring ruins which include the Forum. Its construction began in AD 72 after the Empire suffered a series of civil wars. Its purpose was to subdue the people with a pleasure palace for up to 55,000 spectators and for its inauguration in AD 80 the arena was spectacularly flooded with water for the re-enactment of great historic sea-battles. This was followed by 100 days of circus-style entertainment in which 9,000 wild animals were killed. To encourage attendance, as if any encouragement were needed, spectators were offered free bread.

The entertainment is more dramatically remembered for its gladiatorial contests, where those who were about to die saluted their emperor in his special royal box, and when lions and bears were used in the slaughter of Christians. Unlike many of its neighbouring sites and despite its frivolous purpose, the Colosseum survived remarkably. The Emperor Constantine, who converted to Christianity in AD 312, had the Arch of Constantine built opposite the Colosseum in AD 315. It was tolerated by later Christian leaders who made it a monument to martyrs of the faith. Its fame spread to Britain, where St Bede, an 8th-century monk, proclaimed: 'When the Colosseum shall fall Rome shall fall and when Rome falls the world shall fall.'

BELOW *Second only to the Basilica of St Peter as Rome's top attraction, the Colosseum has survived plunder and the ravages of time to become a symbol of the city's eternal appeal*

LEFT *Where emperors leave their mark: the AD 315 Arch of Constantine, which overlooks the Colosseum, is decorated with reliefs from bygone ages depicting the Empire's great military triumphs*

ABOVE *All roads lead to Rome and in Rome itself many lead to the seat of government — as testified by this excavated and restored road sign on the Via della Curia near the Forum*

House of Vestal Virgins

The House of the Vestal Virgins has the grandeur of a somewhat decayed noblewoman looking out from her beautifully manicured gardens towards the reincarnated city beyond. She looks well, retaining the features of her youth and, with the aid of the archaeological equivalent of Botox, a great deal of her beauty. So does the city. Both are testimonies to the ancient engineers who built them to last and the fervent efforts of later historians, builders and archaeologists who found them and restored them to glory.

The excavations revealed not only the fabric of a great civilization but, in some cases, the lives of the people. The Vestal Virgins were a cult of women aged from six to 36 years who were servants on earth of Vesta, the goddess of hearth and household. Contrary to popular imagination, perhaps encouraged by Hollywood depictions of the excesses of Ancient Rome, they were not scantily-clad dancing nymphs but chaste nuns and their home was effectively a convent.

Friends, Romans, Countrymen

Whereas the Colosseum has survived in all its glory into the tourist age, a great many of the ruins of Ancient Rome, like the House of the Vestal Virgins, had originally disappeared almost without trace. *Almost*. It is said that shepherds used the area around the Colosseum as pastureland which covered the tumbledown treasures. The uppermost protrusions of the ruins were regarded as mere rocks to provide the shepherds with shelter. Excavation would eventually reveal these to be the tops of columns and arches in a valley flanked by the Palatine and Capitoline Hills. But it was only in the 20th century that it vaguely began to resemble a reconstruction of the ancient city, its streets and even street signs. This was the very heart of the Empire: the seat of government, the Senate House (*Curia*), palaces, temples and an open-space-cum-market-place which evolved into a meeting place whose name became a byword for formal discussion of matters of public concern — the *Forum*, or *Il Foro Romano*. Although there were hundreds of *fora* in cities throughout the Empire, this was the largest of them all. And it was here, according to Shakespeare, that Mark Antony delivered his memorable 'Friends, Romans, Countrymen' oration after the assassination of Cæsar.

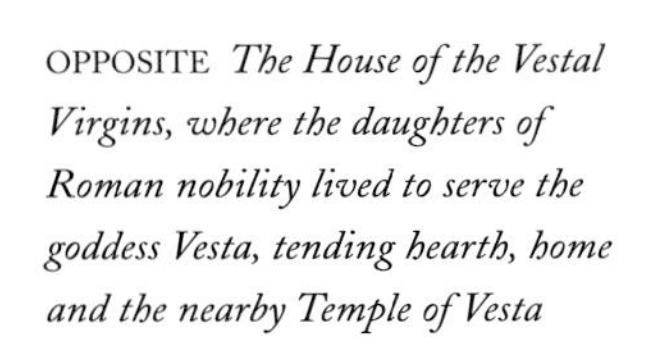
OPPOSITE *The House of the Vestal Virgins, where the daughters of Roman nobility lived to serve the goddess Vesta, tending hearth, home and the nearby Temple of Vesta*

Museums & galleries

Rome is a museum unto itself. All roads lead to the past, and every pavement, piazza or pathway is a journey into history. The museums themselves are but points from which to start the journey, or incidental wayside ports of call — and some might qualify merely as signposts along the way. There are a great many of them. Count up the number of Roman museums in a handful of different guidebooks and no two of them will agree on exactly how many there are. So it's as well to start the journey with those that metaphorically qualify as *major termini.*

Foremost among these is unquestionably the Capitoline Museum complex in the ancient city, set in two palaces designed by Michelangelo to the east and west sides of the Piazza del Campidoglio. Their treasures include a wealth of antique sculptures in bronze and marble, tapestries, porcelain and paintings as well as Greek and Etruscan vases. Famously they are home to the fragmented remains of a vast statue of Emperor Constantine, whose surviving head stands at about 8ft (2.5m) high. This and other fragments form part of a Roman 'Colossus' which once stood 40ft (12m) high. The museum's exteriors are every bit as glorious, with massive Corinthian pilasters and Ionic columns, and a courtyard fountain from the 2nd century AD depicting the reclining river god Marforio.

Also numbered among the unmissable museums of Rome are the Roman National Museum and the Villa Borghese Museum Park. The Museo Nationale Romano, to use its formal title, has sites throughout the city but is based at Piazza dei Cinquecento. It has what is rated as one of the world's most important archaeological collections, which includes the Baths of Diocletian from AD 306. Villa Borghese, once a vineyard to the north of the city, is now a 200-acre park (80 hectares) with five museums, gardens, lakes, fountains and a deer park. Now Rome's largest public park, the original vineyard was transformed by a nephew of Pope Paul V, Cardinal Borghese, into a pleasure palace in the early 17th century.

On this journey into the past many smaller museums catch the eye. Among these is the Keats-Shelley Museum in Piazza di Spagna, dedicated to the Romantics. It was the poet Robert Browning who said: 'Every one soon or late comes round by Rome.'

ABOVE *Bernini's baroque masterpiece sculpture of David (1623–24) at his mightiest as he prepares to hurl the stone at Goliath, housed in the Galleria Borghese*

LEFT *The impeccably preserved full-length statue of the river god Marforio on a fountain in a courtyard at Rome's palatial Capitoline Museum complex*

OPPOSITE *A head of his time. Some of the fragments of the giant 4th-century statue of Emperor Constantine, originally 40ft (12m) at its full height*

RIGHT *The curving colonnade of one side of the elliptical St Peter's Square, known in Italian as Piazza di San Pietro, which stands at the front of the Basilica*

OPPOSITE *The opulent and spacious interior of St Peter's Basilica in the Vatican. Peter (Petrus in Latin) was the rock (petram) on which Christ founded his Church*

BELOW *A pikestaffed soldier of the colourfully-uniformed Swiss Guard who have been a presence in the Vatican since the 15th century*

The Vatican & St Peter's Basilica

The Vatican is a city within a city: in its time, and arguably even today, more powerful than the Italian capital itself. It has all the trappings of a city-state, with its own newspaper, radio station, heliport and police force. It is a glistening memorial to the triumphs and excesses of the Renaissance and the hub of worldwide Catholicism. It is also a cenotaph to the martyrs of the very faith upon which the Vatican is founded. Its centrepiece is the Basilica of St Peter and the crowning glory of this holy diadem is its dome, designed by Michelangelo but not completed in his lifetime. It is visible all over the city and farther afield but, curiously, it can't be seen from St Peter's Square.

Built by Bernini, the square is elliptical with a central obelisk and surrounded by two colonnades formed of 284 columns in four rows, with Swiss Guards at one end. The colourfully-costumed mercenaries, famed for discipline and loyalty, have been guarding the Vatican since the 15th century and are visible throughout the enclave. They were chosen because, in any theoretical war with Rome, it was unthinkable that Roman should take arms against Roman. The interior of the Basilica is radiant with eye-dazzling opulence, and its sheer size — capable of accommodating the population of a town of 60,000 — is breathtaking The interior of the dome is the setting of the famous quotation of Christ when he 'annointed' St Peter as his successor on earth: *Tv est Petrvs et svper hanc petram ædificabo ecclesеam meam. Tibi dabo claves regni cælorvm* (Thou art Peter and upon this rock I will build my church… I will give unto thee the keys to the kingdom of Heaven).

Beyond the Basilica there is a great complex of palatial buildings that house the Vatican Museums. It is a maze of galleries and rooms that have accumulated priceless works over the centuries which today represents the world's greatest art collection. Part of the museum is the Sistine Chapel, whose frescoed ceiling by Michelangelo is probably the climactic culmination of any visit. His scenes from the Book of Genesis are considered to have the most awesome depictions of God ever undertaken by an artist.

RIGHT *One of the giant twin fountains in Piazza Farnese outside the Palazzo Farnese. The marble of the fountains was plundered from ancient Roman baths*

LEFT *Volpetti on Via Marmorata, Testaccio, is an Aladdin's cave of goodies including meats, cheeses, olive oils and delicious rustic breads such as the round Roman rosetta, which looks like an open rose, sprinkled with herbs and tomatoes*

BELOW *Courgette flowers for sale at Campo dei Fiori market*

Food & markets

The countryside around Rome has rich pickings of aromatic herbs, glossy vegetables, pungent garlic and prize-winning onions. A feast of sensory delights awaits visitors in the markets, where stallholders shout their wares, advertising everything from plump green artichokes and courgettes attached to their sunny yellow flowers to spices for *pizza erotica* – which needs no translation – to *pecorino*. This straw-coloured cheese belies its creamy white interior and is made from ewe's milk. There are variations in other regions of Italy, but it is from Rome that pecorino orginates. When mature, it is strong and nutty, but an excellent alternative is the glistening white soft ricotta cheese, used in many delicious Roman desserts or *dolci*. Tender, plump globe artichokes fried whole in olive oil, are served to crispy perfection by the Romans. Known as *carciofi alla giudia*, the hard outer leaves are removed and when fried, the petals open up like delicate flowers. The same treatment is given to the yellow courgettes, *zucchini*, flowers.

Of all Rome's markets, the Campo dei Fiori is the oldest – and the most colourful. Translated literally, it means 'field of flowers' when, in the Middle Ages, the area was a meadow. Tradition also says that this 'garden of temptations' also alludes to 'Flora's Courtyard', named after Pompey's mistress during the time of Julius Caesar. Trysts took on a much darker aura here, too, as the piazza's eternally colourful history includes murders as well as executions. The 16th/17th-century painter Caravaggio is said to have killed a tennis-game opponent on this spot, and the statue of the philosopher Giordano Bruno in the piazza commemorates his being burned at the stake in 1660 for alleged heresy against the Church. Today the Campo dei Fiori is alive with market traders every morning and buzzes after dark with bars and restaurants.

In Testaccio, the famous Volpetti delicatessen delights every sense with its mouthwatering displays of regional delicacies. And when sensory overload is complete, why not imitate the Romans with their art of *dolce far niente* – literally the sweetness of doing nothing – but enjoying a glorious *gelato* from one of the hundreds of traditional ice-cream parlours. It's the perfect Italian way to cool off at any time of the day or night.

OVERLEAF *The famous 'salumeria', Volpetti – the luxurious delicatessen hung with cooked meats and salamis, such as 'corallina', Rome's prized spicy version, and mouthwatering cheeses*

INSIDE *Shoppers from every walk of life come to the 'garden of temptations' that is the Campo dei Fiori market set around the statue of Giordano Bruno*

ZOLA
ITALIA
ROMA
ITALIA

COLTIBUO
BAGOS · DI
BAGOLINO
€98,96
BAGOSS
ESTIVO
MALGA BRUFFIONE
LAGHETTI
Nostri Vini Novelli
FICHI CALABRESI
31,00
79,00
FROMAGGERIA

ANGIOLETTI DI NORCIA
PANNERONE

Alimento
al farro
LOTI

LEFT *Glorious gelato – ice-cream cones at a 'gelateria' near the Trevi Fountain, Rome*

The fountains of Rome

When it comes to basic human functions like eating, the Romans, well, make a feast of it. When it comes to love-making, the word *romance* says it all. So it's no surprise that, when dealing with the most prosaic of human needs — plain drinking water — they again excel themselves, turning it into a ritual embroidered with art and beauty.

Water has been something of an obsession with Romans since ancient times, when no fewer than 11 aqueducts supplied the city with thousands of gallons daily. But it wasn't until the Renaissance that the proliferation of fountains got underway. Today, Rome has more fountains than any other city in the world. Many are small and ornamented by little more than fern-fringes. In palatial estates they are shamelessly called *nymphæums* and echo the cascades of the nymphs' grottos. Some fountains, like the matching pair in Piazza Farnese fronting the Palazzo Farnese, have immense historical pedigrees. Originally part of a 3rd-century Roman bath they were installed at the palace in the 17th century.

The most famous Roman fountain is the Fontana di Trevi. An 18th-century creation, it has beguiled itself into the lore of the city. The baroque-style edifice featuring divinities and a chariot driven by Tritons and water-horses attracts millions of visitors. Traditionally they throw in two coins. The first is for any personal wish. The second is to guarantee the wisher's return to the *Eternal City*.

BELOW *Wishes and horses and chariots of foam against a vast edifice — the Trevi is the star among Rome's 4,000 fountains*

Northwest Italy

Soaring mountains, flat plains, Italy's largest seaport, picturesque villages perched precariously over the Mediterranean, chic Riviera towns and the elegant former capital of Savoy combine to make this one of Italy's most diverse regions.

The Valle d'Aosta and Liguria are the smallest provinces in northern Italy. While the Aosta Valley is surrounded by Europe's highest Alpine peaks, Liguria is where Alps and Apennines converge, ultimately plunging into the Mediterranean. Straddling France and Italy, Monte Bianco (Mont Blanc) is Europe's highest mountain, but the loftiest entirely within Italy is the Gran Paradiso at 13,321ft (4,061m) from which the country's first national park takes its name. Once the royal hunting reserve for the House of Savoy, this is now a *paradiso* for animals, birds and rare flora.

Along the coast, squeezed between mountain and sea, is big, salty Genoa, the birthplace of Christopher Columbus and capital of Liguria. On either side stretches the 200-mile (322km) 'Italian Riviera' coastline. To the west the flower-filled Riviera di Ponente meets the French border, while to the east the Riviera di Levante encompasses chic Portofino and the five quintessentially Riviera villages, the Cinque Terre.

Set dramatically against the amphitheatre of the Alps, Turin is the capital of Piedmont and economic powerhouse of the north. Famous as the home of Fiat, it is also an understated, graceful city with splendid museums and beautiful baroque architecture.

Set among terraced vineyards, clinging to the towering cliffs over the Ligurian Sea, Manarola is one of the most picturesque of the Cinque Terre

ABOVE *Colourful, compact rows of tall houses grace and protect the waterfront at romantic Portovenere, the ancient coastal town that was once prey to pirates*

Cinque Terre

Five picturesque villages set among terraced hills make up the UNESCO World Heritage Site, Cinque Terre. Lord Byron described this 12 miles (20km) of sheer, rocky coastline, sprinkled with vineyards and olive groves, as 'paradise on earth'. At the westernmost point is Monterosso al Mare, the largest of the 'famous five'. From here, an ancient coastal footpath, the Sentiero Azzurro links the main villages. Vernazza, the prettiest of all, is cupped around a sheltered cove with a labyrinth of back streets full of craft and wine shops. The next village, Corniglia, set high on a ridge, is the smallest and, unlike the others, is inland. Known as a farming and vine-growing community it is famous for its full-bodied white wine *schiacchetrà*. On foot it takes about an hour to the fishing village Manarola and from the eyrie at the top of the mountain there are magnificent views of all the villages. A lemon-tree-scented path, the Via dell'Amore (Lovers' Lane) winds down to Riomaggiore, one of the larger villages, carved into the tumbling hillside.

Portovenere

Also a UNESCO World Heritage Site, Portovenere sits on a rocky peninsula in the Gulf of La Spezia, southeast of the Cinque Terre. The picturesque church on the promontory was once the site of a temple to Venus (*Venere* in Italian), from which Portovenere takes its name. Now one of the most romantic villages in Liguria, it was not always thus. Originally it was a pirates' lair and when the Genoese bought the village in 1113 as a border post, they fortified it against the worst possible pirate attack. From its upper parts, there are splendid views towards the Cinque Terre and Lerici, beloved of the English Romantics and known fondly as the 'Gulf of Poets'. Lord Byron loved to swim in the waters around here and lived nearby.

LEFT *Colourwashed houses, cafés and boats cluster around the sheltered harbour at Vernazza, probably the prettiest of all the Cinque Terre villages*

BELOW *Small, colourful boats tied up in Vernazza, the only one of the five villages that has a tourist port*

LEFT *The spectacularly located Vernazza amid steeply terraced vineyards and meadow flowers, clinging to the cliff with the sea sparkling below*

Genoa

As Italy's largest seaport, Genoa (*Genova* in Italian) has often been seen merely as a departure point or somewhere to pass through quickly en route to the resorts of the Italian Riviera. Yet this city, dubbed *La Superba* (the proud) by the early Renaissance scholar Francesco Petrarch, was home to the great explorer Christopher Columbus, to the great admiral of the Genoese fleet, Andrea Doria, to the Italian freedom fighter Giuseppe Mazzini, to the great violin virtuoso, Niccolò Paganini and has been the inspiration to countless artists, poets and writers. Among its famous sons today is Renzo Piano, one of the world's greatest architects who made his name by co-designing the Pompidou Centre in Paris with Richard Rogers and who has transformed the old port in the city.

In 2004 Genoa reigned as 'European Capital of Culture' and the effects linger on. At its heart lies a fine medieval centre to rival any in Europe. The *caruggi,* the classic city alleyways in the old town (*centro storico*), are punctuated by treasure-filled churches and stylish boutiques. Historically the richest part of the city, the *Porto Antico* (old port), is also the most modern and is the site of Europe's largest aquarium. For centuries Genoa sought its fortune on the high seas and was once their master. Even the name probably originates from the Latin *iuana* meaning access from the mountains to the sea. Countless poets and artists have called it 'the city of a thousand colours'. Balconies, terraces, frescoed façades, loggias and hanging gardens are suffused with the sparkling light flooding in from the sea.

For years a long rivalry existed with Venice, as the cities fought to control the Mediterranean trading routes. Surprising and contrasting, where splendid palaces dwarf the tiniest of alleys and where the land is spread over a mountain plunging down to the sea, this great seaport is now worthy more than ever of its title, *La Superba*.

OPPOSITE *The characteristic black and white stripes of Ligurian churches here displayed in the 12th-century Gothic façade of the Duomo San Lorenzo*

BELOW *Porto Antico, restructured by Renzo Piano and Piano's rotating panoramic lift 'il Bigo', which offers stunning panoramic views over the city and sea*

Parco Nazionale Gran Paradiso

In the Aosta Valley, close to Mont Blanc on the border with France, is the Gran Paradiso – the only mountain whose summit reaches over 13,123ft (4,000m) that is totally within Italian territory. Vittorio Emanuele II of Italy created part of the Gran Paradiso as his royal hunting reserve in 1856 to protect the wild goat, and he also created a network of paths and mule tracks for his foresters. In 1922, 173,000 acres (7,0000 hectares) of this patch of heaven became Italy's first National Park – a glorious landscape of meadows, valleys, glaciers, waterfalls and high Alpine beauty.

The king and symbol of Gran Paradiso is Europe's largest Alpine mammal, the ibex (*stambecco*), a powerfully-built mountain goat with long, curved horns. Its smaller cousin, the chamois, is also a permanent member of the park along with foxes and ermines. So, too, is the Alpine marmot, the largest squirrel species, which usually announces itself with a loud whistle, especially when the resident Royal eagles wheel menacingly overhead.

The Gran Paradiso is criss-crossed with about 450 miles of mule-tracks and marked trails and sprinkled with *rifugi* (mountain huts), where many walkers stay during the summer months. As well as spotting the resident wildlife, trekkers can expect to be accompanied by clouds of colourful butterflies and sightings of rare Alpine flowers. The very attractive valleys of Cogne and Valnontey are the main access points to this earthly paradise.

LEFT *The dramatically-sited Valley of Valnontey has excellent access to the footpaths of the Gran Paradiso National Park*

Riviera di Levante

Named after the rising sun, the eastern coast of Liguria stretches from Genoa to La Spezia. The rugged landscape, where mountain meets the sea, has produced a hardy race of Ligurians who have scratched a meagre living from rock and sea for thousands of years. Yet the unique geography has produced a landscape and climate more apposite to the more southern reaches of Italy. The terraced land is redolent of citrus fruits, vines and olives punctuated by swaying palm trees. And while the Ligurians still make a living from the bounty of *il mare* (the sea) and *la terra* (land), the lure for tourists of the jewels of the Riviera di Levante such as the Cinque Terre and Portofino have increased their wealth exponentially.

Portofino

This former fishing village is the Italian Riviera's über-exclusive resort. The world's rich and famous have made it into a millionaire's playground building on its fame since Roman times and its 'discovery' by the British in the 19th century. Often imitated – by Portmeirion in Wales, for example – it is still the *numero uno* for those seeking an ultra-discreet escape, far from the more brash territory across the border in France. Surrounded by silvery olive groves and pines, the semi-circular waterfront is lined with pastel-coloured houses with frescoed façades and flower-filled roof terraces. In front of the harbour the cobbled piazzetta is awash with cafés, restaurants and fabled A-list designer shops such as Giorgio Armani and Dolce & Gabbana, many of whose owners have shuttered villas peeping out over the scene.

The Promontory of Portofino is a protected nature reserve where, away from prying eyes, there are splendid cliffside walks along paths strewn with aromatic herbs and wild flowers, high above the azure sea. And from the harbour there are boat rides along the coast to the Cinque Terre, to the main resorts of Camogli and Rapallo and to nearby Santa Margherita Ligure – less exclusive, more affordable, but also idyllic.

RIGHT *From huge, millionaires' yachts to traditional wooden fishing vessels – whatever floats your boat in Portofino*

L'ANCORA
CONFEZIONI
15 GE836D

21

Riviera di Ponente

'The spot on the horizon where the sun sets' is the meaning of Ponente. Stretching from the French border to Genoa, the Riviera di Ponente is a thin strip of coastal plain framed by Alpine foothills. From elevated viaducts and snaking roads, the resorts and marinas far below seem but mere specks in a glorious panorama of glittering sea reflected in acres of glasshouses. For this stretch of coastline is also an area known for its great production of flowers and is often nicknamed the 'Riviera dei Fiori'. Blooms proliferate in the temperate climate and many greenhouses raise cut flowers in this, the centre of Italy's flower industry.

The air is perfumed with the scent of the roses, mimosa and carnations that are exported and seaside towns, such as Diano Marina, are famous not only for the pleasures of the beach, but also for the late spring flower festival, the *Infiorata*, when the streets are covered with petals. The most famous of the resort towns along this side of the Riviera is San Remo, which not only has its famous Art Nouveau casino and elegant old hotels, but also has a charming medieval centre.

As well as seaside resorts, in the background there are countless old villages steeped in the atmosphere of the past, such as charming Porto Maurizio with its huddled houses and narrow streets in the province of Imperia. Imperia was once divided by the Imperio river – the medieval Porto Maurizio was up on a hill on the west side of the river delta and the more modern Oneglia to the east. After centuries of bitter rivalry the two communities were joined in 1923. Oneglia had always been a harbour for the House of Savoy while Porto Maurizio's loyalties were to Genoa, 70 miles (112km) away to the southwest.

LEFT *The popular seaside resort of Diano Marina, Queen of the 'Riviera dei Fiori'*

OPPOSITE *Part of the labyrinth of medieval alleyways in Porto Maurizio, Imperia*

Turin

Famous as the home of Christianity's most important relic, the Turin Shroud, Turin was also praised by the French architect Le Corbusier as 'the city with the most beautiful natural location'.

Turin put the letter 'T' into Fiat (*Fabbrica Italiana Automobili Torino*) and the 'Italian' into the classic film, *The Italian Job* – but this is much more than a city of cars and the birthplace of Italian cinema. Set against the backdrop of the natural amphitheatre of the Alps, it has royal palaces, baroque castles, elegant boulevards and 11 miles of portico walkways fit for a king. Indeed, it was the seat of the House of Savoy and became the first capital of the Kingdom of Italy in 1861.

Today, in addition to its 40 museums, it is also the design and contemporary art capital of Italy. And, for a slice of the *dolce vita*, Turin is a gourmet paradise and birthplace of the Italian cinema, long before lights first flickered in Rome's Cinecittà studios.

Looming above the rooftops is the city's icon – the soaring spire of the Mole Antonelliana. This Art Nouveau folly is now home to the fascinating National Museum of Cinema. As the birthplace of the Italian cinema industry and faithful to its enduring love affair with film, the city today has a higher proportion of cinema screens to inhabitants than any other Italian city and hosts the annual International Torino Film Festival – Italy's largest film festival after Venice.

Elegant shops grace the city, which also has the only Hermès designer shop in Europe that discreetly packages its luxurious purchases in plain white, unmarked bags, so avoiding any fashion statements. The Versace store had to close – perhaps it was a little too flashy and ostentatious for this understated city.

Café society is alive and flourishing in Turin. Whether it's the regal, chandeliered charm of the historic Caffè Torino, the historic Baratti & Milano, or the Caffè San Carlo – a famous hang-out of the philosopher-poet Friedrich Nietzsche – you'll always be assured of drinking good coffee in Turin. And, for lovers of chocolate, this is the Italian capital where it was first popularized in 1678.

LEFT *Turin and the landmark Mole Antoniella, framed by the celestial amphitheatre of the snowy Alps*

BELOW *Ingot-shaped 'gianduiotti' studded with hazelnuts are every chocoholic's idea of paradise at Caffè Baratti e Milano*

Lombardy & Emilia Romagna

Plains, lakes, mountains, cities of art, gastronomy, designer chic and the economic heart of the country are the splendours of this region.

Rome may be the capital of Italy, but Lombardy's Milan is the most prosperous. This was the city in which Leonardo da Vinci lived and worked for 20 years and which boasts the world's largest Gothic cathedral. It has given us the famous La Scala opera house and is the headquarters of matchless Italian style and fashion gurus.

Lombardy is the cradle of Romanesque architecture and each city is endowed with beautiful examples. Bergamo is a delightful town, which has what many believe to be the most picturesque piazza in the country. And, in Emilia Romagna, Bologna earned its nickname 'La Grassa' (the fat) as the gourmet capital of Italy.

The French writer Stendhal famously pitied 'those who are not madly in love with the Italian Lakes' and even Sigmund Freud was quite potty about them. Languorous, sophisticated, star-struck, set among jaw-dropping scenery, the sparkling lakes continue to seduce and bewitch, just as they have for centuries.

Majestic Lake Maggiore is lined with graceful villas and has the beautiful Borromean Islands in its midst. Como is the deepest and, some say, the most achingly romantic. Today it is also a hideaway for Hollywood celebrities and, as the closest lake to Milan, it is also the business capital's playground.

Detail of the soaring spires of Milan's Duomo. There are 135 of them adorning the world's largest Gothic cathedral

Bergamo

Perched on cypress-clad hills, Bergamo is a refreshing retreat from the Lombardy plains. It is divided into the historic *città alta* (upper city) and the modern *città bassa* (lower city). The walled upper city is a tangle of cobbled streets, medieval spires, bars and shady piazzas, all of which reflect the influence of the Venetian empire, which ruled from 1428 to 1797. At its heart is the Rocca fortress, built by the Venetians for protection from the Milanese.

The centrepiece of the *città alta* is the Piazza Vecchia, a blend of medieval and Renaissance architecture, believed by many to be Italy's most picturesque piazza. The 12th-century Palazzo della Ragione, or law courts, bears the proud statue of the Lion of Venice.

The Palazzo's portico connects Piazza Vecchia with the little Piazza del Duomo (named after its cathedral), the

RIGHT *The ornate Colleoni Chapel, built into Santa Maria Maggiore church, Piazza del Duomo*

BELOW *Medieval Palazzo della Ragione from Piazza Vecchia, with the Lion of Venice visible above the central window*

Romanesque church Santa Maria Maggiore, and the Colleoni Chapel. The ornate baroque interior of Santa Maria Maggiore belies its austere exterior and within is the tomb of Bergamo's fêted son, Gaetano Donizetti. This prolific composer wrote 71 operas, 18 symphonies and dozens of other works before dying in his home town in 1848, aged just 51 years.

Next door is the colourful Colleoni Chapel – a masterpiece of Lombard art. This early Renaissance, fabulously ornate edifice was completed in 1476 at the behest of the legendary soldier of fortune, Bartolomeo Colleoni, for his tomb.

Linked by funicular, the lower town (*città bassa*) was laid out around the beginning of the 20th century, and is composed of a number of pleasant wide boulevards. Its highlight is the Accademia Carrara, which holds one of the greatest collections of Lombard and Venetian art including works by luminaries such as Tintoretto, Mantegna and Bellini. It is also the site of a very good museum of contemporary art.

ABOVE *View over the rooftops of Bergamo with distant vistas of the Lombardy plains, Bergamo hills and pre-Alp mountains*

Bologna

Surrounded by hills, the capital of Emilia Romagna is a harmonious blend of warm, russet-red brick, arcaded walkways, wide piazzas and elegant palaces. Its many nicknames include *La Dotta* (the Learned) – the seat of Italy's oldest university (1088) – *La Rossa* (red) – for both its politics and its red-coloured buildings – and for its love of gourmet and gourmand delicacies.

The adjoining squares of Piazza Maggiore and Piazza del Nettuno form the nucleus of the city. Giambologna's 16th-century bronze statue of Neptune in his eponymous piazza towers over an ornate fountain, which is the city's symbol. In baroque times the modesty of the scandalously proportioned sea god was protected by a pair of bronze trousers – revealingly removed in more liberated times.

The Piazza Maggiore's imposing, unfinished cathedral, the Basilica di San Petronio, is the world's fifth largest church and is counted among Italy's finest medieval brick buildings. The first stone was laid in 1390 as the start of a grand plan to rival St Peter's in Rome in size, but work was abandoned in 1650 and the funds were used instead for the building of the university.

South of the Basilica is the university's first official building, the Archiginnasio, of Europe's oldest surviving university. It was within these walls that the instruction in the dissection of human bodies was first introduced in the *Teatro Anatomico*.

In this city of piazzas and porticoes, of which there are 25 miles (40km), pride of place goes to wonderful food shops and family-run restaurants. 'Bolognese' sauce needs little introduction and is at its authentic best in Bologna, but never served with spaghetti – tagliatelle is the proper accompaniment. The making of pasta is elevated to an art form here and *tortelloni* (pasta parcels) are lovingly sculpted. The corpulent native composer Giacomo Rossini was perhaps a little too fond of this delicacy. And, within the region, the king of cheeses Parmigiano-Reggiano (Parmesan), Parma ham and balsamic vinegar from Modena all have spectacular starring roles.

ABOVE *Via Calzolerie greengrocer, one of many 'fast food outlets' in gourmet capital, Bologna*

OPPOSITE *Giambologna's Fontana del Nettuno (Neptune's Fountain), adorned with putti, dolphins and mermaids, crowned by the floodlit muscular bronze figure of Neptune in Piazza Maggiore*

RIGHT *View of Cannero Riviera with ferry, at the foot of Mount Carza, Lake Maggiore*

OPPOSITE *Archway over a flight of steps at the entrance to the sub-tropical gardens at Isola Madre, Isole Borromee (Borromean Islands)*

BELOW *Statuary soaring over the rooftops and gardens of the Palazzo on Isola Bella, Isole Borromee (Borromean Islands)*

Lake Maggiore & Borromean Islands

Lake Maggiore is the second largest of the Italian Lakes (after Lake Garda). Covering an area of 132 square miles (212 square km), it borders Piedmont on the western shore, Lombardy in the east and noses north into Switzerland. Known as *Lacus Verbanus* in Ancient Rome, fragrant verbena still grows on its shores and the Mediterranean-style climate allows all kinds of exotic plants to flourish. Framed by snow-capped mountains, this is where northern Europe meets the Alps and the warm welcome of Italy. It is said that the waters of the lake are composed of the teardrops of unrequited lovers and romantic poets. Stendhal, Byron, Shelley and Wordsworth were all seduced by its beauty as, later, was Ernest Hemingway, invalided here during World War I in the luxurious Grand Hotel des Iles Borromées, which he featured in *A Farewell to Arms*. The shores are lined with palatial villas – the hideaways of 19th-century aristocrats.

Rising from the waters in the heart of the lake are the three enchanting Borromean islands. The English historian and writer Edward Gibbon was moved to describe them in his *Memoirs* (1796) as 'an enchanted palace, a work of the fairies in the midst of a lake encompassed with mountains, and far removed from the haunts of men'. Isola Bella especially was already known as the lush pleasure island of the Counts Borromeo – then, as now, the property of the Milanese Borromeo family. Isola Bella is a masterpiece with ornate gardens and a gilded baroque palace full of Murano chandeliers and frescoes. The baroque Italian garden, laid out over 10 terraces, filled with rare and exotic plants, adorned with fountains, grottoes, statuary and dramatic perspectives, is constructed in the form of a pyramid crowned by a huge statue of a unicorn, ridden by Love. The larger Isola Madre (mother island) is like a floating sub-tropical garden, where pure white peacocks strut alongside pheasants and vivid parrots. It is famous, too, for its spectacular display of azaleas, rhododendrons and camellias and for the Kashmir cypress – more than 200 years old and the largest example in Europe.

Lake Como & Bellagio

Shaped like an inverted 'Y', Lake Como is the deepest, most scenically dramatic and varied of all the northern lakes. Known as *Lacus Larius* in Roman times, when Pliny the Roman general had two villas here, today it is still referred to as 'Lario'. Many say it is the most romantic lake, including Shelley, Byron and Wordsworth, who described it as 'a treasure which the earth keeps to itself'. Como has long been admired by celebrities from Greta Garbo to the late fashion designer Gianni Versace. It was here, according to locals, that President Kennedy romanced Marilyn Monroe and, since George Clooney bought a large stretch of waterside, Lake Como is once again bathed in Hollywood glamour. Still in fashion, too, is the *passeggiata* (the ritual of the evening promenade).

Out on the silky lake, steamers gently carving their wakes in the reflection of snow-clad peaks still stir visitors, as does the view from Ossuccio – one of the most romantic vistas of the lake. Opposite, Como's only island, the green Isola Comacina, shimmers like a precious emerald. One of the earliest settlements on the lake, pre-Roman times, it is now an artists' colony and site of an exclusive restaurant. But cradled between the two arms of Como's 'Y' shape is Bellagio, the most prestigious and picturesque resort. From its glittering headland there are magical views of the long, slender lake. The labyrinth of lanes and cobbled streets are the perfect place for a leisurely stroll, with enticing shops whose wares include gorgeous silky accessories, for which Como is so famous.

BELOW *The fabulous view across Lake Como to Bellagio, with the mountains in background*

LEFT *View of Lake Como from Ossuccio, with the 11th-century church of SS Giacomo and Filippo and its famous sail-shaped bell tower in the foreground, looking out towards Isola Comacina*

Milan

The unofficial capital of Italy, Milan started life as a modest city on the Lombardy plain. Its fame began to rise under the Romans, who called it *Mediolanum* (middle of the plain), reflecting its key position between the trade routes of northwest Europe and Rome.

The heart of the city is the Piazza del Duomo, dominated by the world's largest Gothic cathedral, begun in 1386 under Gian Galeazzo Visconti. This dazzlingly white marble confection has flying buttresses, gables, gargoyles and 135 spires – the highest of which is crowned by the gilded statue of the *Madonnina,* the city protector, soaring 358ft (109m) high. The Duomo is Europe's third-largest church after St Peter's in Rome and Seville's Cathedral. The highlight is a visit to the roof for bird's-eye views of the intricate detail on the marble statues, of the Madonna and, on a clear day, as far as the Alps.

A mere stroll away is the glass-domed Galleria Vittorio Emanuele II, full of designer shops, chic cafés and restaurants. Nearby is the world-famous opera house, La Scala – restored to its former opulence under twinkling chandeliers. Just around the corner is the Quadrilatero – or designer district – studded with native Prada, Versace, Dolce e Gabbana among the glamorous, legendary names. A little further out of the centre is the earlier design guru's masterpiece, Leonardo da Vinci's 15th-century *The Last Supper* (*Il Cenacolo*) – one of the world's most famous works of art in this city devoted to matchless Italian style.

ABOVE *Galleria Vittorio Emanuele II, the glass-domed arcade designed by Giuseppe Mengoni, who tragically tumbled from the roof's scaffolding the year before its opening in 1877*

LEFT *Intricate carved detail on the marble statues and some of the 135 spires viewed from the rooftop of Milan's Duomo, the world's largest Gothic cathedral*

HOTEL MARCONI

Venice

More than any city in the world, Venice has captivated, enchanted and seduced every soul who has ever paid court to this elegant lady of the lagoon, perched on 118 individual islets separated by 150 channels and linked by 400 bridges. Its aura has launched writers into eulogies, lifted artists to great heights of visual inspiration, and has drawn droves of film-makers to its bosom. It's an astonishing fact that a city standing on larchwood rafts and timber piles has survived for 13 centuries. Few would dispute that 'La Serenissima', as it was known, is the most beautiful city in the world, but its popularity puts the city in danger of becoming a purely visual phenomenon. And of demeaning a great city once heaving with 200,000 Venetians. The native population of Venice has dwindled and on any day it is outnumbered by tourists and service-industry workers from the mainland.

Still, even though it's in danger of falling victim to its own overwhelming beauty, it will never be said that Venice didn't know how to put on a good show. The canals and their bridges, the churches and palaces, the museums and galleries, the magnificence of St Mark's Square and its great bell tower – surrounded by enticing restaurants as well as the Basilica di San Marco and the Doge's Palace – are all the stars of the show. Not forgetting the annual spectacular in which the city comes to life in human form during the Venice *Carnevale*. In the 10 days before Lent, Venice is transformed by a glittering, frenzied pageant of masquerades and revels.

A view of the Grand Canal From the Rialto Bridge, lined with busy bars and gondola platforms with candy-stripe poles

Basilica di San Marco

PAGE 49 *The dazzling array of domes, arches, portals, spires and statuary that comprises the magnificent hotchpotch of the Basilica di San Marco in Venice*

BELOW *A pigeons' eye-view of the lavish interior of the Basilica, with its Greek-cross-style layout and glorious mosaics depicting the New Testament*

Everything spectacular that happens in Venice is never very far from the city's vast Piazza San Marco (St Mark's Square), with its dramatic campanile (bell tower) which can be climbed for some spectacular views, and columns bearing the figure of the winged lion, which is the symbol of Venice. The square is the scene of the greatest revelry during the Venice *Carnevale* and a huge focal point for the 18 million tourists who make an appearance in Venice every year. This is largely because the square is overlooked by two of the most elaborate buildings in Venice — the Doge's Palace (Palazzo Ducale), and St Mark's Cathedral (Basilica di San Marco).

The present cathedral is based on an original that was built in the 9th century as home of the discovered remains of St Mark, the gospeller. After a fire it was replaced in the 11th century by the building we see today. Inside and out it presents the observer with a serious case of sensory overload. Its magnificence is beyond question but, as Charles Dickens said when he saw it, 'opium couldn't build such a place'. It is a hotchpotch of styles and designs which emerge as something largely Byzantine and Greek Orthodox with some Roman and Hellenic touches. The effect is stunning but confusing.

The interior of the Basilica is marginally more orderly, designed in the shape of a Greek cross and with mosaics covering some 43,000 sq feet (4,000 sq metres) of the wall-space. It depicts the events of the New Testament from the beginning of Christianity to the Last Judgment. There are also mosaic pavements showing pictures of birds and beasts, some of them mythical. The glittering effect goes some way to explaining why St Mark's is called *Basilica d'Oro* — the Golden Church.

LEFT *A colourful Venetian masquerader watching rather than being watched*

OVER *The spectacularly floodlit Rialto bridge. On the last day of the Venice Carnival, revellers traditionally carry fiery torches through the streets of the city in a glittering pageant, and there are marvellous firework displays*

INSIDE *Revellers wearing colourful costume and theatrical masks for the annual Venice Carnival*

Carnevale

Lord Byron, who spent three fruitful and fun-packed years in Venice around 1819, once said: 'A man only reveals himself when wearing a mask.' What the womanizing aristocratic-poet thought about women in masks isn't recorded, though he no doubt loved many of them.

The wearing of masks is at the heart of the Venetian *Carnevale* – the Latin expression for fasting, meaning 'farewell to meat' – which has been an annual event in Venice for nigh on a thousand years. Hedonistic to the point of debauchery, the mask ritual was a 10-day release from the constraints of behaving as one ought. It allowed nobility to mix with the lower échelons of society or even to change sex. Masked aristocratic ladies might act out their fantasies with a gondolier, and a maidservant might dress as her mistress. Often they would adopt characters of lore – favourites among which were Harlequin (*Arlecchino*), with his large nose and red lump on his head, and Harlequin's master, the miserly merchant Pantalone. There are also fantasy masks like the white-sculpted *maschera nobile* (noble mask), worn with a black coat and tricorn, or the *Columbina,* which is an elaborately plumed eye-mask. Some of the masks can be quite sinister, like the Plague Doctor mask which resembles a mournful vulture with a long beak.

The very first Venice Carnival is thought to have taken place in the year 1094 and by 1458 the revelry had become so debauched that a decree was announced forbidding men from entering convents dressed as women to commit *multas inhonestates* (much disgrace). In the 18th century it had evolved into a licentious two-month party, but Napoleon's invasion put a stop to it and things didn't really get going again until 1979.

Traditionalists say that the modern version is a tame affair but it remains a glittering pageant of costumes, parades, parties, concerts and fireworks. On the opening day San Marco is thronged with masqueraders and general feasting. It comes to a close on Shrove Tuesday, when revellers gather for a masked ball and torch-bearing masqueraders run amok, illuminating the city. Quite a spectacle, reflected in the shimmering waters of the canals.

BELOW *A formal procession of Venetians in historical costumes for the Carnival*

EMPO

EN VERVS FORTIS QVI FREGIT VINCVLA MORTIS

ABOVE *One of the four evangelists adorning the gable of the Church of San Giorgio Maggiore seems to gaze out across the Giudecca Canal towards San Marco*

RIGHT *The architectural masterpiece of Andrea Palladio on San Giorgio Maggiore — a first impressive glimpse of the beauty of Venice's churches for visitors arriving by sea*

Churches

Across the water from San Marco, there's an island quite remote from the main part of Venice called San Giorgio Maggiore – home to a majestic church of the same name. Apart from the architectural importance of the very highly rated Renaissance church, it has a natural prominence as the first Venetian building visitors see when approaching the city by sea – and it whets their appetite for the glories of the more central churches. It was designed and started by Andrea Palladio in 1566 but was not completed until after his death. Bathed in white though sometimes a little pinkish at certain times of a sunlit day, the frontage bears the statues of four evangelists. Among some excellent paintings within there is *The Last Supper*, perhaps the most famous work by Tintoretto (1518-84).

Salvation and thanksgiving

In any good travel guide to Venice, anything upwards of 80 churches will be listed. You may not be able to find them all but there are some you really must see. If the idea of what keeps Venice afloat fascinates you, then visit the Basilica di Santa Maria della Salute – usually called the 'Salute' – kept above water by a million timber piles.

The church of Il Redentore (formally Chiesa del Santissimo Redentore, or Church of the Holy Redeemer), like the church of its neighbouring island, San Giorgio Maggiore, came into being on Giudecca at the hands of Andrea Palladio in 1577. The white-domed Il Redentore, with its statue of the Redeemer, is regarded as one of the highpoints of Palladio's career. The church was built in thanks for the end of the plague that had ravaged Venice two years earlier. The government later instituted a thanksgiving mass on the third Sunday in March, which survives to this day. These days, as then, worshippers and dignitaries cross a quarter-mile stretch of canal to the island from the main Venice area of Zattere by temporary pontoon bridge. The whole affair begins the night before, when St Mark's basin fills with thousands of boats joining in the festivities amid a huge fireworks display.

LEFT *The white-domed Il Redentore, crowned by a statue of the Holy Redeemer, was built in the 16th century as a thanksgiving for Venice's deliverance from the plague that killed 50,000 citizens*

HOTEL RIALTO
HOTEL

LEFT *The neo-Gothic canal-based Pescheria fish market, near the Rialto Bridge, is barely 100 years old but there have been fish markets on this site since the 14th century*

BELOW *Inside the busy and colourful fish market, one of the great attractions in this part of Venice on the Canal Grande*

Rialto

Of the six districts (*sestieri*) of Venice, the two most bustling areas are the political *sestiere* of San Marco and the commercial district of San Polo, which is also the location of Venice's first and most important bridge, Ponte di Rialto. The bridge takes its name from the locality around it on the city's 'main street', the Grand Canal – an area originally known as *Rivo Alto*, or 'high bank'.

This is where Venice becomes a living city, with its people going about their business. It just happens that their workplace is the most famous canal in the world. And although it's a hugely popular tourist spot, this native heart of the city is primarily a market area and a traditional commercial centre where visitors will hear very little but Italian spoken. Even so, the tourists come in their droves to see the great arched bridge, snap photographs of the gondolas and *vaporetti* (water buses), maybe have a snack or a coffee at an old-fashioned canal-side bar, or visit the tempting stalls of the markets. The *Erberia* (fruit and vegetable market) is a lively sprawling affair and the *Pescheria* (fish market) is located in a rather quaint neo-Gothic building dating back to 1907, although there have been fish markets hereabouts since the 14th century. Years ago, when the market area around the Rialto was known as the 'bazaar of Europe', it was a much more lavish affair dealing in exotic goods including spices and fabrics. In its centuries of existence it has been the home of the real life merchants of Venice, as well as the setting for the Shakespeare play of that name – and it was the location of the first Italian state-owned bank.

Built in 1592, the stone-built, single-span balustraded construction, lined both sides with shops, replaced wooden drawbridge structures dating back to the 12th century. Before 1854, when the first Academia bridge was built, the Rialto was the only place to cross the Grand Canal.

OPPOSITE *The 16th-century Ponte di Rialto, Venice's first and most famous bridge in a bustling area where the canal and surrounding markets, bars and hotels come to life*

OVERLEAF *Never does Venice better live up to its name, 'La Serenissima', than at night time, when the Rialto gleams over now-serene waters and the gondolas have taken to their quiet moorings*

onese
Venezia, Museo Correr
13.II - 29.V.2005

Museums & galleries

Just along from the Rialto bridge by water bus is the 13th-century Ca' d'Oro, the House of Gold, a beautiful Gothic Palace that gets its name from the gold leaf that originally adorned its walls. Today, it houses Galleria Giorgio Franchetti's excellent collection of Venetian art, though the star of the show is the famously gory *Martyrdom of St Sebastian* by Andrea Mantegna (1431-1506).

Serious gallery-browsers won't want to miss the big name galleries like the Accademia, Venice's top art museum with a collection spanning five centuries, and the Guggenheim Collection of Modern Art. There are dozens more, some more specialized than others, but the one that nobody can miss is the Doge's Palace (Palazzo Ducale) in St Mark's Square. This magnificent building, one-time home of the Doge of Venice and the seat of government when the city was an independent republic, has been well preserved. Its collections of paintings and sculptures include all the great names of Venetian art. The most dazzling and biggest of its great chambers is the Sala del Maggior Consiglio, where the Great Council used to meet. Among its art decorations is one that's thought to be the largest painting in the world —*Paradise,* by Tintoretto, about 25 x 81ft (7.45 x 24.65m).

The Palace was also a court of law with a direct link to a prison at the rear via the so-called Bridge of Sighs (Il Ponte dei Sospiri). The evocative name echoes the despair of convicted prisoners as they were taken away.

RIGHT *Inside the Sala del Maggior Consiglio (Great Council Room) of the Doge's Palace. Its eastern wall has what is thought to be the largest painting in the world*

BELOW *Among Venice's rich collections of art galleries and museums is the splendid Ca' d'Oro (House of Gold), which overlooks the Grand Canal*

Northeast Italy

Bordered in the north by Switzerland, Austria and Slovenia and in the south by a trio of art cities, this is also the region of Italy's most dramatically beautiful mountain range and of its largest lake.

Sandwiched between mountain and lake is the fertile plain of Veneto and the lovely cities of Verona, Padua and Vicenza. The second biggest city after Venice, Verona was known in Roman times as 'Little Rome'. Today, it is still famous for its magnificent Roman arena, romantic Renaissance gardens and as the 'home' of Shakespeare's star-crossed lovers, Romeo and Juliet.

Nearby, the old university town Padua is one of Italy's most popular sites of pilgrimage to see Giotto's luminescent fresco cycle in the Cappella degli Scrovegni.

Equidistant between Verona and Venice is elegant, Renaissance Vicenza – birthplace of Andrea Palladio, Italy's leading 16th-century architect.

Seemingly as wide as a sea, Lake Garda was the first lake to be discovered by 'Grand Tourists'. Here the vine and citrus tree-clad plains of the southern reaches are in dramatic contrast with the untamed north, ringed by snow-capped peaks that embrace and protect from the cold north winds. The jagged towers, lonely pinnacles and giddily steep faces moved the famous French architect Le Corbusier to name the Dolomites 'the most beautiful natural architecture on earth'.

And, as the sun sinks in its fiery glow during the *enrosadira* when all the Dolomiti peaks turn pink, it is hard to disagree with that emotion.

Statuary in the Giardino Giusti, gardens of the Palazzo Giusti laid out in 1580 – one of Italy's finest Renaissance gardens

Dolomites

The Dolomites is a mountain range in the Italian Alps in the Trentino-Alto Adige/Südtirol region, with the neighbouring Veneto rising to 10,965ft (3,344m).

Geologically very different from the main body of the Alps, the crenellated spires, soaring towers and jagged peaks of these spectacular pink-tinged mountains lend a surreal feel to this most beautiful of landscapes.

An 18th-century French mineralogist Déodat de Dolomieu gave the name 'Dolomite' to these mountains, with their magnesium-rich rock that resembles limestone. When the region was covered by the tropical sea some 230 million years ago, the accumulation of coral, algae and marine invertebrates created islands and mud flats. Erupting volcanoes spewed lava into the sea, which cooled in the gaps between the 'tropical' islands, leaving behind the dark brown volcanic rock still visible today in places such as Val di Fassa and Val Gardena.

Yet while the Dolomites were named after a Frenchman, it was the British who were the first to demystify them. British mountaineers waxed lyrical about the grandeur of these glorious peaks in their alpine journals in the 19th century. In 1837, John Murray Publishers produced a guide to the Alps which mentioned the existence of the Dolomites for the first time in print. This was the spur that sent so many British mountaineers to explore the Dolomites for themselves, and led to the founding of the Alpine Club of London (now Great Britain), the first alpine association in the world.

It is also a winter sports paradise, with one of the world's largest ski areas covering 758 miles (1,220km) of pistes served by over 450 state-of-the-art lifts. Close to the Austrian border, Teutonic efficiency blends harmoniously with some of the best mountain restaurants found anywhere in the Alps. In the land of the *dolce vita*, the Italians know that a good lunch set among stunning scenery is just as important as the skiing. Outside the ski season, meadows full of alpine flowers recall a vision of Heidi heaven.

RIGHT *View towards Canazei village and across to La Marmolada glacier and Grand Vernel mountains in Val di Fassa, Trentino*

RIGHT *Statue of Juliet at the Casa di Giulietta (Juliet's House), Via Cappello, Verona*

Verona

'There is no world without Verona walls' cries Romeo, confronting the prospect of banishment from the city and his beloved Juliet. Fêted by performance, quotation, parody, school curricula – and, not least the tourist industry – *Romeo and Juliet* lives on in the streets of romantic Verona. Sighing lovers are drawn by the magnet of the Casa di Giulietta (Juliet's House), its marbled balcony and romantic courtyard. It may be a fictional shrine, even if the warring Montagues and Capulets did actually exist, but why let authenticity get in the way of one of the world's most romantic and tragic plays?

Long before Shakespeare set his story of the star-crossed lovers in Verona, this was a Roman city, much of which still survives, notably the Porta dei Borsari and Porta dei Leoni gates and, above all, the Arena. Dating from the 1st century AD, the interior of this vast amphitheatre has survived virtually intact. It is the third largest in the world after Rome's Colosseum and Santa Maria Capua Vetere (near Naples). In its heyday it accommodated up to 25,000 spectators, who came for the 'entertainment' of watching combats to the death between gladiators or men and wild beasts in a bloody circus, to the cries of *Jugula!* (Slit his throat!). Today's audiences come to be dazzled by Italy's most theatrical open-air operatic festival in the summer months.

Handsome pink-tinged limestone *palazzi* line the banks of the River Adige, hewn from the local *rosso di Verona* stone. Contained within massive 16th-century walls, the harmonious blend of Roman, medieval and Renaissance influences combine to make this a picturesque, mellow city, full of treasures. It was the birthplace of Veronese, the great Venetian painter, and of Catullus, the Latin lyric poet, who penned so many love verses in the 1st century BC. Then as now, this is a timeless city for lovers.

ABOVE *Tourists in the courtyard of Juliet's House, Verona, looking up towards the crowded balcony*

LEFT *The Roman gate Porta dei Borsari, near Corso Cavour, at night*

Vicenza

Lying about midway between Verona and Padua, Vicenza is one of Veneto's wealthiest cities and is also world-famous as the city of Palladian architecture. Countless villas dot the surrounding countryside and many *palazzi* in the city centre.

The Renaissance architect Andrea Palladio is often described as the most influential and most imitated architect in the Western world. He particularly admired the monuments left by the Ancient Greeks and Romans, and often used the orders of classical columns in his buildings. He studied the symmetrical, harmonious forms of those early buildings and brought them back into fashion. He designed many buildings and churches in Venice, such as Il Redentore, and the whole city of Vicenza is a showcase for his work.

Andrea was born in Padua in 1508, the son of Pietro della Gondola. At 13 he became an apprentice stonemason and then left for Vicenza. He met nobleman Giangiorgio Trissino, who decided to put him under his protection, changing his name to the more classical-sounding Palladio (meaning 'sacred to Pallade Athena').

Five hundred years after his birth, Andrea Palladio is still one of the world's best-known architects, his influence reaching down through the generations from English architect Inigo Jones and American Thomas Jefferson to the present day. The City of Vicenza and the Palladian villas of the Veneto are UNESCO World Heritage Sites. The massive, green-domed Renaissance town hall, now called the Basilica Palladiana, was Palladio's first major triumph. The revolutionary design encased the original Gothic palazzo within a two-storey loggia. Many of Palladio's villas are outside the city, such as Villa Caldogno in the province of Vicenza. He always designed his villas in context with their setting. If situated on a hill there were views in all directions – such as the Rotonda, the most famous of all Palladian villas.

His last remarkable work, the Teatro Olimpico, was begun in the year of his death in 1580 and finished by Scamozzi five years later. Built of wood and stucco, this was a classical outdoor theatre created inside a medieval fortress building and is the earliest surviving indoor theatre of modern times.

OPPOSITE *Palladio's Villa Caldogno, Via Pagello – detail of decoration with female statues and frescoes by Gianantonio Fasolo and Battista Zelotti*

BELOW *UNESCO World Heritage Site Teatro Olimpico – the world's oldest surviving indoor theatre*

RIGHT *Looking down over the rooftops to the colourful town centre of Riva del Garda, dominated by its tall clock tower*

BELOW *Fishing boats at Torri del Benaco, eastern side of Lake Garda*

Lake Garda

Lying apart from the other Italian lakes, Garda is the largest and most scenically diverse. It stretches from the Lombardy Plain to the foot of the Trentino Dolomites in the north, where mountains rise straight from the shoreline. Every afternoon in summer, the cooling breeze of the Ora funnels down from the Brenta Dolomites and on to Lake Garda. The northern reaches resemble a deep Norweigan fjord, narrow and enclosed between towering mountain ranges. Those peaks and pinnacles protect the flourishing olive trees, palms, oleanders, camellias and citrus fruits in this extraordinarily mild climate, known to the Romans as Lake Benacus, the 'beneficient'.

At the northern end, Riva del Garda has always been a favourite of writers and poets such as D H Lawrence, Stendhal and Goethe, who called it a 'miracle of nature'. The town's Roman origins and medieval core of little streets are clearly visible, as are the reflections of snowy peaks shimmering in the turquoise waters.

On the eastern shore, brightly coloured boats cluster around the little port at Torri del Benaco, which lies on the Riviera degli Olivi (the Riviera of olive groves). And just to the south, Bardolino is cradled among hills cloaked with vineyards that produce the lusty red wines of this area.

At the southernmost point is the scenic walled town of Sirmione, set on a peninsula protected by the 13th-century castle, Rocca Scaligera. The poet Catullus (87–54 BC) named it the jewel of 'almost islands' and it was here that he died after writing so many of his love poems – 'Vivamus, mea Lesbia, atque amemus…' (Let us live, my Lesbia, and let us love…)

LEFT *The Scaligera Castle, Sirmione, on the southern end of Lake Garda*

BELOW *Boats in the harbour at Bardolino on the eastern side of Lake Garda*

Padua

Wealthy Padua (Padova as it's known in Italian) has been a flourishing university town since the Middle Ages. It was one of the locations in Shakespeare's *The Taming of the Shrew* but, most famously, it is the site of pilgrimage to see Giotto's superb fresco cycle and visit the shrine of Sant'Antonio (St Anthony).

On 13 June every year thousands of pilgrims flock to the 13th-century Basilica di Sant'Antonio. St Anthony is the patron saint of Padua, but he is also the patron of childbirth, the poor – and lost property. Byzantine domes and minarets decorate the exotic exterior, reminiscent of Venice's St Mark's, while inside the cathedral the tomb of St Anthony is hung with votive offerings. The surrounding walls are adorned with marble reliefs charting scenes from his life, and the high altar has a magnificent series of reliefs by the Florentine Renaissance artist and sculptor Donatello, depicting the miracles of St Anthony.

But many art lovers flock to Padua just to visit the Scrovegni Chapel (Cappella degli Scrovegni). 'An uninterrupted tapestry… calm, azured, starred like a fine clear sky' enthused the 19th-century French writer Théophile Gautier over the frescoes by the great Florentine artist, Giotto. Paduan nobleman Enrico Scrovegni built this small chapel to atone for his father's sins, commissioning Giotto to decorate it between 1303 and 1305. The resulting fresco cycle is celestial, covering the walls from floor to ceiling with jewel-like colours enhanced by softly burnished hues, bathed in the cool blue light of the chapel. Dedicated to the Virgin, the Life of Christ and the Last Judgement, this is the most complete medieval fresco series still intact and marks the break with the preceding Byzantine tradition.

In the heart of the town, Roman remains, medieval palaces and Renaissance squares all vie for attention in elegant yet lively Padua, which, along with Bologna and Florence, has the distinction of being one of Italy's most important centres of learning.

RIGHT *The Basilica di Sant' Antonio, which is dedicated to Padua's patron saint, St Anthony, dates from 1232 and is one of Italy's top pilgrimage sites*

Florence & Tuscany

The popularity of Florence and Tuscany is epitomized by its very British appellation as 'Chianti-shire'. Its attraction is self evident – as home to the arts and the modern concept of politics, and as a major historical destination whose civilization predates the rise and fall of Ancient Rome. The highly refined Etruscan civilization dominated northern and central Italy, largely between the Arno and Tiber rivers, until the 5th century BC and the area was known to the Romans as 'Etrusci' – from which derives the name of the modern Italian region of Tuscany. Later, what had become an obscure Italian backwater re-found glory as the home of the artistic apocalypse that we call the Renaissance. Its burgeoning influence transformed the modern world in the shape of buildings like the Duomo of Florence. The architecture of the time defied the geometric creations of the ancients, and the art introduced character and teased humankind's secret sense of the erotic.

Tuscany is dotted with time-capsule little villages, towns and cities like Lucca, Siena, Pisa, Arezzo and San Gimignano. The region is also the home of a Tuscan archipelago, of which the most familiar member is the Island of Elba.

Nowhere more epitomizes the artistic reincarnation of the Renaissance in Europe than its Tuscan birthplace. In the plain language of the author D H Lawrence, Tuscany represented the 'end of the old world and the beginning of the new'.

Florence's sumptuous landmark, the Duomo, serves as a bold yet elegant milestone on the road pioneered by the great minds of the Renaiissance

Florence churches

The 'flower' of Florence's churches and the city's crowning glory is, figuratively and literally, the Duomo. Formally known as the Basilica di Santa Maria del Fiore – which translates as St Mary of the Flower – its dome (cupola) is visually stunning and its construction rewrote the handbook of architectural geometry. Architect Filippo Brunelleschi (1377-1446) created it out of four million bricks on a unique octagonal base. Inside the Duomo is a vast collection of Renaissance treasures, with sculptures by Michelangelo. Elsewhere the nearby Museo dell'Opera del Duomo, originally little more than a site office from where work on the Basilica was overseen, is now home to the museum, and a vast repository of Duomo 'overspill', including Michelangelo's *Pietà* and Donatello's original *Cantoria* (choir-loft). Another room has the original Duomo organ balcony, with panels depicting choirboys, by Luca della Robbia (1400-82).

Like the Duomo, many of Florence's churches evoke an inside–outside rivalry between external architectural magnificence and the treasures and beauty of the interior. A case in point is the Church of Santa Maria Novella, which began life back in the 11th century but had to wait until the 15th century to re-emerge in its full re-consecrated beauty with its white marble façade, tinted with green and pink. The interior treasures include its pulpit, designed by Brunelleschi, from which the 'heretical' astronomer Galileo Galilei was denounced.

To see more of the work of Brunelleschi, it is worth looking beyond the splendid exterior of the Basilica of Santa Croce (Holy Cross) to the stylish architectural lines of Cappella dei Pazzi within. On the way to and around the chapel there are famous works including some by Donatello, Giotto and British sculptor Henry Moore, as well as the tombs of Galileo and Michelangelo.

RIGHT *The glorious façade of Santa Maria Novella basks in its elegant symmetry, overlooking a flower-fringed piazza in the northwestern corner of central Florence*

Ponte Vecchio

Along with the *Duomo* of Florence — and perhaps also the original and many replicas of Michelangelo's *David* – the most instantly recognizable image of the city is its Ponte Vecchio, literally the 'old bridge'. The 14th-century bridge isn't just a fragment of the past. It is an inhabited part of daily life in Florence as it was in the beginning – a river crossing and a shopping centre rolled into one. It wasn't the first bridge on this site. It replaced a series of bridges that disappeared or were swept away by floods.

Joining both sides of the River Arno at its narrowest point, the present Ponte Vecchio was originally covered and occupied by food shops. But at the end of the 15th century the butchers and others were evicted by the Medici, who installed highly respected silversmiths and goldsmiths in their place. Several prominent Florentine artists worked in gold, including Donatello and Cellini whose statue is in the middle of the bridge. The railing around the unfortunate Cellini bust eventually fell victim to a lovers' craze. It's said that couples who secure a padlock attached to some part of the bridge (usually the railing) and throw the key into the river will stay together forever. Fearing for the fabric of the bridge with all those padlocks being removed, the authorities outlawed the lovers' ritual on pain of a hefty fine.

One aspect of the bridge that has changed from the original was the building of Corridoio Vasariano. This was a secret corridor, designed by the artist and historian Vasari at the end of the 16th century to link the Palazzo Vecchio (Town Hall) and the Uffizi building with the Pitti Palace on the other side of the river, via a covered passage on top of the bridge. Remembering that Niccolò Machiavelli was a son of this politically active city, one can only speculate on what nefarious transactions were once conducted between the Uffizi and the Palace. Today, at least, the Uffizi is just a splendid art gallery with unsurpassed views of the river and the city.

ABOVE *One of the many jewellers' shops which have been on the Ponte Vecchio since the butchers were banished in 1593*

OVERLEAF *Silhouetted in the sunset, the bridge is both a dramatic spectacle and a super vantage point for viewing the rest of the city*

INSIDE *The triple-arched stone-built Ponte Vecchio, Florence's oldest bridge, has a secret past but is now an upbeat tourist attraction*

LEFT *A section of the bridge showing the backs of shops and workshops of goldsmiths, silversmiths and, today, art dealers*

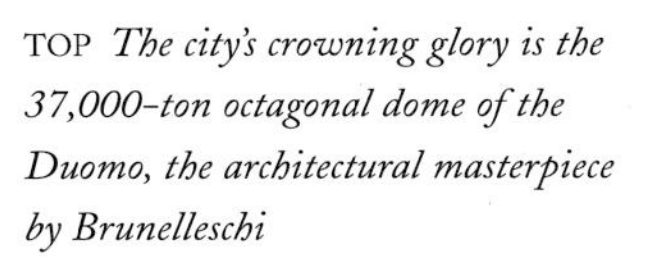

TOP *The city's crowning glory is the 37,000-ton octagonal dome of the Duomo, the architectural masterpiece by Brunelleschi*

ABOVE *Choirboys in a bas relief panel from the original Duomo organ balcony, now part of the Museo dell'Opera del Duomo*

LEFT *The interior of the Cappella dei Pazzi within the Basilica of Santa Croce is a statement of artistic style and design*

Florence galleries

There are galleries in every nook and cranny throughout Florence and virtually every building open to the public has works of art on display. Its place as the cornerstone of the Renaissance has assured the city's status as probably the world's greatest art centre, and a No.1 tourist destination, attracting over six million visitors a year. Aside from the many great works by Italian Renaissance artists located elsewhere in the world – among them, Da Vinci's *Mona Lisa* in the Louvre in Paris – Florence has the greatest concentration of works by the best-loved Renaissance artists of all time, along with some of their most memorable works, including the David statues by both Michelangelo and Donatello, Botticelli's *Birth of Venus* and Da Vinci's *Adoration of the Magi*. The brightest stars in Florence's dazzling constellation of galleries are undoubtedly the Medici Chapels, the Academy, the Palazzo Pitti and the Uffizi Gallery. Foremost of these is the Uffizi, which is among the world's greatest.

Galleria degli Uffizi

Uffizi means, simply, 'the office' – a building that began life as a government bureau built by Giorgio Vasari in 1560 at the behest of Cosimo I de' Medici. Even then, certain rooms were set aside as a gallery which grew by generation until the 18th century, when the collection was bestowed on the city. The building's interior is exquisitely styled and some corridors are works of art in themselves. The 45 rooms are variously given over to different artists in chronological order, though some get more space than others. Botticelli (1445-1510), for example, occupies most of the merged rooms 10-14, whereas the artist he was apprenticed to, Filippo Lippi (1406-69) – who painted the memorable *Madonna And Child With Two Angels* – merits barely one room. A fascinating feature of the Uffizi is the Corridoio Vasariano, a passage leading from the gallery down the banks of the River Arno to the Ponte Vecchio to the Palazzo Pitti over the river.

ABOVE *A detail showing the head of the Madonna from Filippo Lippi's* Madonna and Child with Two Angels *which forms part of his work on show in Florence's Uffizi Gallery*

OPPOSITE *One of the corridors in the Uffizi, once an elegant government office commissioned by Cosimo I – now rated the finest picture gallery in the whole of Italy*

LEFT *A view from the River Arno of the Uffizi and the Corridoio Vasariano, a 'secret' passageway to the Palazzo Pitti across the river*

Museums & galleries

BELOW *The 14ft (4.3m) marble depiction of the Biblical figure, David, by Michelangelo, in Galleria dell'Accademia*

Unbeknown to some people, the museums of Florence do extend beyond pictures, statuary and architecture to include a number of alternative displays – of archaeology, ceramics, science, zoology, anthropology, history and pre-history, among others. There is also a museum called Dante's House, devoted to the life and work of the Florentine poet, Dante Alighieri. But it remains true that the majority of Florence's museums are very grand extensions of the galleries, and those that are museums in their own right are few and far between. You can get your bearings by climbing the beautifully marbled, 278ft (85m) 14th-century Giotto bell tower (*Campanile di Giotto)* next to the Duomo, which affords some beautiful views. From there you can see the spire of the ancient Benedictine monastery of Badia Fiorentina close by the 13th-century tower of the Palazzo del Bargello. Once a police HQ and a prison, the Bargello is now home to the National Museum, which has one of the most impressive collections of Renaissance sculptures in the world — including the 'other' David, by Donatello. The statue of David that everyone comes to Florence to see is in the Galleria dell'Accademia, some distance to the north of the city centre, but well worth the trek if only to catch sight of Michelangelo's magnificent statue of the giant-killer.

The Palazzo Pitti, across the river from the Uffizi, is by contrast a museum district in itself. As well as royal apartments, which include chambers used by members of the Medici, Lorraine and Savoy dynasties, the palace and pavilions of the Giardino di Bóboli have no fewer than eight museums. The most interesting is the Galleria Palatina, a treasury of over 1,000 paintings with works by Titian, Raphael and Caravaggio. There are also rooms dedicated to the planets, including one called the Sala di Marte (Hall of Mars), depicting warlike images including a fresco on the arched ceiling showing the *Triumph of the Medici*, by Pietro da Cortona (1596-1669).

ABOVE *The view from Giotto's bell tower of the tower of Palazzo del Bargello in parallel with the spire of the Badia Fiorentina Benedictine monastery*

LEFT *The sumptuous fountain in the grounds of Palazzo Pitti, which is south of the River Arno and home to the Galleria Palatina*

OPPOSITE *One of the planet-themed rooms within the Palatine Gallery, showing the ceiling fresco of the* Triumph of the Medici *by Pietro da Cortona*

Tuscany

Even among the Tuscan gems of Florence and its sister seats of culture, which include Lucca, Siena and Pisa, there's no shame in seeking respite from the relentless bombardment of the senses by artistic superlatives. The English writer Laurie Lee, who wrote *Cider With Rosie*, said the cities of Tuscany made his eyes become 'choked with pictures and frescoes' and that he subsequently began to 'long for those cool uplands, that country air, for the dateless wild olive and the uncatalogued cuckoo'.

Tuscany occupies a vast area of Italy just above the 'knee' of this boot-shaped land, bordered by the sea to the west and the Apennine mountains to the east. At the centre of the region there is a long, fertile valley called the Valdichiana, where the vineyards yield to acres of olive groves and sunflower fields, and where once-fortified villages and small towns cling to the slopes on either side. The familiar poplar-lined roads meander and weave between meadows where long-tailed sheep graze among fields of camomile and rosemary. Since the days when the poet Shelley described this land as 'a paradise for exiles', Tuscany has been a favourite of foreign visitors, but especially the English. American visitors shouldn't feel offended about being referred to as '*Inglese*' – it's a term they use for all non-Italians, even French and Russians.

Like many communities of an expanding region whose population has spilled down from the hillsides to form a modern part of town more accessible to outsiders arriving by train or motor car, the town of Arezzo still retains its medieval heart and soul. It has the remains of a Roman amphitheatre and its fair share of museums and old churches with artistic treasures. Those that are most prized are a set of frescoes in the 13th-century church of San Francisco called *La Leggenda della Vera Croce* (The Story of the True Cross). There's also a monthly antique market that brings in the visitors. But at its heart Arezzo – like its many neighbours – is a simple market town, built on a hill with sloping streets and piazzas that exude a sense of cool, fresh air for city-weary travellers.

ABOVE *Domestic life seen through a green shuttered window in a typically small Tuscan town in the valley called Valdichiana*

OPPOSITE *On the first weekend of every month, Arezzo's streets and town squares, including Piazza Grande, are overrun by buyers and sellers at the antique market*

LEFT *Renaissance artist Piero della Francesco's masterpiece,* The Story of the True Cross *in Arezzo's church of San Francisco*

RIGHT *Two millennia ago it was an amphitheatre, today the Piazza Anfiteatro of Lucca is a colourful medieval-style market place*

OPPOSITE *A red-brick archway in the 14th-century Case dei Guinigi complex overlooking the Tuscan roofs and towers of Lucca*

Lucca

BELOW *Built on the site of an ancient forum, the spectacularly intricate Romanesque church of San Michele in Foro, topped by a statue of the archangel*

Lucca is an elegant town 50 miles (80km) west of Florence where its courteous 100,000 inhabitants prefer bicycles to cars. Lucca pays a deferential homage to its mixed past as a Roman settlement, an agrarian village, a banking centre, a regional capital and a Renaissance architectural site. All that goes some way towards explaining the wide appeal of the town – among visiting Italians if not the outside world, whose tourists are more likely to be drawn to the attraction of neighbouring Pisa. Classical enthusiasts can revel in its Roman roots going back to the 2nd century BC, among the fragmented remains of a once-great amphitheatre, and the orderly grid-like street plan which survived into the Middle Ages. Music buffs come here in their droves to visit the house of Giacomo Puccini (1858-1924), the composer of operas including *Tosca* and *Madame Butterfly*, who was born and lived here. Country-lovers with an eye for urban beauty can gaze upon Lucca's inner attractions while strolling two-and-a-half miles (4km) along the medieval ramparts which were transformed into a tree-lined promenade in the 19th century. And Lucca is very handy for the seaside – Versilia, a string of coastal towns on the Tuscan Riviera, is about 10 miles (16km) away.

The historical centre of Lucca has a number of architectural gems including the Duomo di San Martino, Piazza Napoleone, the main shopping centre along Via Fillungo, Piazza Anfiteatro, Casa dei Guinigi and the church of San Michele in Foro. Although there's little left of the amphitheatre – much of the stonework was used to build later churches – the square remains a lively location for markets and Casa dei Guinigi is a remarkable complex of 14th-century towers and buildings which belonged to a family of merchants who came to rule the city. The church of San Michele in Foro has one of the most impressive façades in Tuscany. Topped by the winged figure of the archangel St Michael, its twisted marble columns have an individuality that sums up the precious jewel that is Lucca.

Pisa

BELOW *The glorious Romanesque four-tiered façade of Il Duomo, the cathedral church of Pisa in the town's Field of Miracles complex*

The Leaning Tower of Pisa started leaning even before it was complete. It was begun in 1173 and had shown a tilt by the time the first three storeys had been completed. Attempts to correct its original lack of perpendicularity only resulted in its lurching the other way, and over the next 180 years or so more corrections led to the structure becoming slightly curved. The final topping was the bell chamber, built at an angle to the base so that it gave the appearance of being upright. The result is that it looks rather like a drunken man whose tilted hat is the only perpendicular thing about him. Over the years, the building has gradually fallen out of alignment by a total of about 15ft (4.5m). Meanwhile, thanks to modern engineering, it has been made safe enough for anyone fit to face the claustrophobic climb up the 298 stairs.

For all the architectural chaos of this site – the neighbouring Duomo and baptistery are also both slightly out of kilter – the Field of Miracles (*Campo dei Miracoli*), as Pisa's ecclesiastical centre is known, is also a miracle of beauty and achievement. The Duomo, built in 1063, is a masterpiece of Pisan Romanesque design, with an arcaded four-tier façade and a huge bronze door on which episodes in the life of Christ have been cast. Its interior is no less impressive. And the circular Baptistery – the third building in the sacred trio and the largest of its kind in Italy – has a beautiful font and a pulpit designed by Nicola Pisano. On the edge of a town whose attractions are somewhat limited, the Field of Miracles ensemble has a splendid aura of isolation generating a breathtaking impact on visitors, be they medieval travellers or 21st-century trippers.

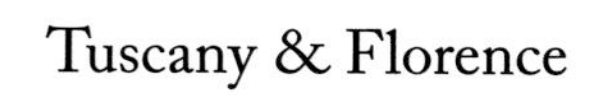

ABOVE *The circular baptistery in the Field of Miracles, the third to be built in the sacred architectural trilogy. It overlooks the Camposanto, Italy's most beautiful cemetery*

LEFT *The spectacular Leaning Tower curves precariously skywards, surrounded by tourist shops and against a backcloth showing the rear of the cathedral*

San Gimignano

This one-time medieval Manhattan's skyline was once overwhelmed by more than 70 towers built in a boastful orgy of pride by prosperous merchants as monuments to their wealth and power. But, sadly, pride came before a dramatic fall when most of the towers were destroyed by envious Florentine rivals in the 14th century. The remaining dozen or so now stand as cenotaphs to the rich past of this most charming and picturesque of the Tuscan hill towns. Known as the 'city of the beautiful towers', Gimignano may have seen its fair share of the Seven Deadly Sins – greed, pride and envy among them – but it evokes nothing but a virtuous warmth, wonder and even passion for those who behold it. For lovers of literature about Italy, the town will be instantly recognizable from its starring role in E M Forster's 1905 novel *Where Angels Fear To Tread*, as the fictional Monteriano. Yet it barely qualifies as a town. You can walk the walls in an hour, and you can cross it in 15 minutes. Even so, it is worth more than a day trip. Apart from the missing towers, its preservation over the centuries is remarkable – the same streets where medieval townsfolk once walked, the same houses where they lived and the same social institutions. See it all from 177ft (54m) and about 200 steps up at the top of the Torre Grossa (the Big Tower), which is the tallest and the only one now accessible, in Piazza del Duomo. Confusingly, there is strictly speaking no Duomo on the site, but there is the Collegiata which the locals refer to as a cathedral. It is admired as the setting for its frescoes of the Bible stories and a chapel devoted largely to pictures of the town's patron saint, St Gimignano, who defended the town when it was under attack from Attila the Hun in the 5th century.

There is no shortage of treasures. In the 13th-century town hall, the Pallazo del Popolo, there hangs a harrowing picture of the Crucifixion by Coppo di Marcovaldo — and a painting by Taddio di Bartoldo showing how Gimignano looked at the turn of the 14th/15th centuries, towers and all. Gaze upon them and weep.

RIGHT *Viewed from the foot of the hill, San Gimignano and just some of the surviving towers of the medieval hill town. Until the 14th century there were 72 of them*

Isola di Elba

What do you do with a world-conquering emperor who has retreated from battle and lost his capital city? Back in 1814 somebody had the idea of sending him on an indefinite vacation to one of Tuscany's attractive little island spots, where he could enjoy an agreeable climate and delightful landscapes among friendly people, get his act together, limit his absence to nine months, raise an army of friendly natives and then get on with the business of taking over the world again. Napoleon Bonaparte may have been in exile, and Elba may not have been his first choice of holiday destination, but he didn't have a hard time here. The island became his own principality which he started to knock into shape, doing some good into the bargain – laying on schools, drainage, overhauling the legal system, modernizing agriculture, building roads and defences. He might have stayed if he'd known that 100 days after his exodus from Elba he would meet his Waterloo and end his life in another exile in the bleaker mid-Atlantic isle of St Helena under the British. Today, Napoleon's two houses on Elba – his main home at Palazzina dei Mulini and his summer villa at San Martino – are huge tourist attractions. Previously the island was valued as a mineralogical paradise, attracting Greeks, Etruscans, Romans and Pisans for ores that could be forged. Today, it's still a favourite with geologists, but it has the additional reputation as a pleasure-ground for sun-seekers and watersport-enthusiasts. It is one of seven Tuscan archipelago islands in the Mediterranean forming Europe's largest National Marine Park. Now if only Napoleon had thought of that…

BELOW *Red roofs in the sunshine, viewed from a hill overlooking the island's attractive and lively capital of Portoferraio*

LEFT AND ABOVE *Napoleon Bonaparte's rustic summer retreat at San Martino, with a close-up of his insignia above the door*

TOP *Working boats rub hulls with pleasure craft in the harbour of the island capital, Portoferraio, near Napoleon's official residence*

Siena

First impressions of Siena are of an entirely self-contained community where everything happens within a relatively tiny cluster of medieval streets. Yes, everything – even horse racing. It seems odd that in among the many functioning buildings and monuments that celebrate an ardent respect for religion and the old ways, there are so many others devoted to equally devout but less sacred pursuits. Like eating, drinking, having fun and even romance. First impressions are, typically, correct, even though their confirmation can become an immense adventure of discovery in this majestic little city.

Established in the 12th century, Siena has a history and culture to rival Florence and a cityscape and municipal rituals reminiscent of the Vatican; it is as fascinating as Rome and Venice – without the tourist hordes.

Siena's Campo is a pristine, scallop-shaped city square towards which all other streets in the city seem to radiate. On two dates in every summer – in July and August – it is the scene of the famous Palio, a bareback horse race three times round the square, where sand is laid for the occasion and mattresses are mounted on walls to offset the possibility of injury. The race, which dates back to the 13th century, when it was originally staged on a circuit through the town, is accompanied, before and after, by a huge amount of ritual, pageantry and inter-parish rivalry.

Overlooking the square is the imposingly elegant Palazzo

BELOW *The Baptistery of Siena's Duomo, with its exquisite hexagonal font with carvings depicting the life of St John the Baptist, surrounded by elaborate frescoes*

Pubblico and the adjacent Torre del Mangia. The tower offers spectacular views of the town and surrounding countryside, while the city hall houses the Museo Civico, which is famous for a great many paintings, including the allegorical frescoes entitled *The Effects of Good and Bad Government* by Ambrogio Lorenzetti (1290-1348). The streets of Siena are enchanting, especially in the older quarter around Palazzo Chigi-Saracini with its curved Gothic walls. The Duomo is a splendid building with a beautiful vaulted ceiling and marble pillars with carved figures representing various Popes. The cathedral baptistery is no less impressive, with a hexagonal font portraying the life of John the Baptist.

ABOVE *A walk at eventide in one of Siena's oldest areas – Via di Città, alongside the curved Gothic walls of the Palazzo Chigi-Saracini*

RIGHT *The Campo – heart of Siena and the setting of the famous twice-yearly horse race – overlooked by the magnificent Palazzo Pubblico and the Torre del Mangia*

Umbria & Le Marche

Umbria is the green heart of Italy, a realm of medieval hilltowns dotted with cypress trees standing sentinel over vineyards and olive groves. It is the only land-locked region of Italy – where soft-contoured hills are bordered by the Apennines in the east in a vision of rural charm. The lesser-known Marche (pronounced mahr-key) region is in the 'calf' of Italy's long, tapering boot, next to Tuscany and Umbria. Here, the towns are on a human scale and life is slow and gentle. The shining star is Urbino – the model of courtly life.

As the capital of Umbria, Perugia has the region's most fabulous art gallery, the largest church, a building that has been called Italy's most beautiful public building, and it is famous, too, for its chocolate *baci* 'kisses'. It also has a fine medieval centre although its heritage goes back further to Etruscan times. Orvieto, known for its crisp white wine, has a tradition of winemaking traced back to its Etruscan origins. Gubbio and Spoleto have been called the loveliest of the Umbrian hilltowns, attaining near perfection in their setting and containing treasure troves of art. And, in this region full of Franciscan stories, Assisi is the birthplace of St Francis, the most popular of saints, known for his love of nature and all God's creatures. Although the Basilica of San Francesco and some frescoes were seriously damaged in the earthquakes of 1997, restoration is complete and the Basilica, with its Giotto paintings, is second only to Rome's St Peter's as the world's most important pilgrimage destination.

View over the rooftops of Perugia with the landmark San Domenico Church – Umbria's biggest church – clearly seen

Urbino

'On the slopes of the Apennines, almost in the centre towards the Adriatic, is situated, as everyone knows, the little city of Urbino'. So says Castiglione, the author of *The Book of the Courtier* (*Il Cortegiano,* 1528) who based his model of courtly life on this town and made it renowned throughout Europe in the 16th century. Urbino's rose-coloured buildings are bathed in golden light high up among the mountains as if in a time warp. At its heart is the Palazzo Ducale, built in the mid-15th century by Duke Federico da Montefeltro and known as Italy's most beautiful Renaissance palace. This elegant blend of serene, harmonious architecture was commissioned by the duke as a tribute to the artistic and intellectual ideals of the Renaissance as well as to courtly life. For the duke and his contemporaries, man was at the centre of the humanist universe – a break with Christian philosophy. In *Il Cortegiano* Castiglione's protagonist defines for the court of Urbino the old Italian term of *sprezzatura* which describes the art of making something difficult look easy or effortless. 'I have discovered a universal rule which seems to apply more than any other in all human actions or words; namely, to steer away from affectation at all costs, as if it were a rough and dangerous reef....and to practise in all things a certain nonchalance which conceals all artistry and makes whatever one says or does seem uncontrived and effortless'.

BELOW *The high, curving external walls of the Palazzo Ducale in Urbino – often called Italy's most beautiful Renaissance palace*

LEFT *Massive sunflower blooms, grown for their seeds and the resultant oil in the rolling agricultural lands of Le Marche*

ABOVE *The Renaissance porch of the lower Basilica di San Francesco, Assisi showing the magnificent rose window guarded by the four evangelists' symbols*

Assisi

The birthplace of the medieval playboy-turned-pilgrim and patron saint of Italy was added to UNESCO's World Heritage Site list in 2000. It is a place of pilgrimage, not only to see the shrine to St Francis and the glorious Giotto frescoes but also to become immersed in the timeless beauty of this pink-tinged medieval town, cradled by the slopes of Monte Subiaso. The son of a materialistic cloth merchant, Francesco (Francis) was born in Assisi in 1182. His early life was dedicated to sybaritic pleasures and womanizing until visions came to him. While praying in San Damiano church, the crucifix bowed, beseeching him to simplify his life and rebuild the Catholic Church. Francis took the message literally, renounced materialistic goods and became a beggar. He exchanged his fine cloth for hair shirts, kissed lepers and embraced a life of poverty, obedience and chastity.

St Francis & the Poor Clares

St Francis founded the enclosed order of the Poor Clares, headed by Chiara Offreduccio, the St Clare whose life and legend became closely entwined with his. The Basilica of Santa Chiara's rose and white limestone Romanesque exterior is supported by huge flying buttresses – generous in their feminine curves. Inside is the San Damiano crucifix, which spoke to St Francis, and the body of St Clare is displayed in the crypt. Glorious in its simplicity, the façade of the Basilica di San Francesco is like the saint that it commemorates and is his resting place. The basilica is two-storeyed – the first stone was laid in the lower part in 1228, the day after Francis's canonization, just two years after his death.

The lower basilica contains some of Europe's most important medieval frescoes, but despite the earthquake damage in 1997, the upper basilica is still the highlight. Giotto's famous fresco cycle, *Life of St Francis* (1290-95) is a miracle of luminosity and revived the art of fresco painting in Italy. For some this larger-than-life church was a betrayal of the saint's faith in humility and poverty, for others it was a statement of the spiritual glory of this larger-than-life person.

Undeniable is the saint's humility and love of all God's creatures, referring to his own body as an 'ass', poverty as his beautiful 'bride' and death as his 'sister'.

OPPOSITE *Basilica di Santa Chiara, dedicated to St Clare, the spiritual soul mate of St Francis of Assisi*

LEFT *View from the rustic tiled roofs of medieval Gubbio looking out to the parapets and crenellated tower of the Palazzo dei Consoli (built 1332–1349) by A da Orvieto*

BELOW *Pedestrians on a steep paved lane walking towards the Palazzo dei Consoli with a row of flower-filled pots decorating a window-ledge in the foreground*

Gubbio

On display in the Palazzo dei Consoli are seven pieces of bronze inscribed with Etruscan and Roman characters. These priceless slabs are known as the Eugubine Tablets dating from 250-150 BC. Gubbio's ancient origins are reflected in its buildings, seemingly as ancient as time, set in a glorious position clinging to the mountainside. Known once as the 'City of Silence' Gubbio is also a perfect medieval town and, many say, Umbria's finest.

The Roman part is on the plain and features a well-preserved Roman theatre dating from the 1st century. Later, the town was sited higher up on the flanks of Monte Ingino and today's focal point is the Piazza Grande crowned by its magnificent Palazzo dei Consoli. This huge building with its crenellated tower is visible for miles around and was begun in 1321 by the architect Angelo da Orvieto and took 200 years to complete. Nearby, the Gothic cathedral lies opposite the Renaissance Palazzo Ducale. Designed as a smaller scale version of Urbino's Palazzo Ducale by the renowned Duke of Urbino, Federico da Montefeltro, this is the expression of a lifestyle inspired by the humanistic civilization. Federico was born near Gubbio and St Francis of Assisi also lived for some time in this town. Legend has it that there was once a fierce man-eating wolf that terrorized the townsfolk. Francis went into the hills in search of the wild animal, made the sign of the cross and addressed the salivating beast courteously as 'Brother Wolf', at which point it closed its jaws and lay down at his feet. Francis led the wolf into the town where, surrounded by startled citizens, he won a pledge because the wolf had 'done evil out of hunger'. The townsfolk were to feed the wolf regularly and, in return, the wolf would no longer prey on them nor their flocks. Freedom followed and Francis, always the animal lover and medieval animal rights activist, even made a pact on behalf of the town's dogs that they would not bother the wolf ever again.

Passions are always inflamed in May for the annual 900-year-old race at Gubbio, the 'Corsa dei Ceri'. Enormous wooden candles (*ceri*) are borne aloft in frenzied races, culminating in much feasting and drinking. Whether Christian festival or pagan ritual, there is no mistaking the very phallic aspect of the 'ceri'.

OPPOSITE *Palazzo dei Consoli, Piazza Grande, Gubbio*

Orvieto

Formerly an Etruscan settlement, ancient walls surround medieval Orvieto, which sits on an outcrop of volcanic cliff. Long ago, volcanic outpourings made these lands fertile, creating a favourable situation for the vines that produce Orvieto's famous white wines.

The huge Piazza del Duomo has its eponymous cathedral at its heart, described by Pope Leo XIII as 'the golden lily of Italian cathedrals', as it appears to float to Heaven. It was built by papal decree to celebrate the 'Miracle of Bolsena', when in 1263 drops of blood seemingly flowed from a consecrated host on to an altar chalice cloth during Mass at a church in Bolsena, near Orvieto. Work started in 1290 and continued for 300 years but the end result is one of Italy's greatest Romanesque-Gothic cathedrals. The 14th-century façade glitters with sumptuous mosaics against horizontal bands of dove-grey tufa and white travertine. Inside, the floor is made of ox-blood coloured marble and the Cappella di San Brizio houses astonishing frescoes by Luca Signorelli in the Last Judgement cycle (1499-1504) which influenced Michelangelo's later version in the Sistine Chapel. Overlooking the Duomo is the Museo Claudio Faina – a showcase for one of Italy's most important archaeological collections including Etruscan artefacts dating back to the 4th century BC, echoing Orvieto's ancient origins. At the foot of the town among vineyards, apple and peach trees is the Etruscan necropolis, the Crocifisso del Tufo, where stone chamber tombs are laid along a rectangular street grid. Vineyards stretch as far as the eye can see. Traditional Orvieto Abbocato was a sweet wine matured in the caves cut into the tufa volcanic stone and renowned for its excellence. Today's Orvieto Classico is drier and crisper.

LEFT *Distant view of Orvieto*

RIGHT *Bottles of the local wine of Orvieto, produced on the terraces around the ancient Umbrian town*

Perugia

This venerable university town has a lovely medieval centre and, like Orvieto, was originally an Etruscan settlement. The intact Etruscan arch, Arco Etrusco, is the gateway to the centre and labyrinth of alleyways so narrow that, it is said, lovers can lean out and kiss across them. For, as well as being the capital of Umbria, Perugia has given the world millions of *baci* – chocolate 'kisses' filled with nougat cream. And in October, lovers of chocolate throng the Corso Vannucci for Eurochocolate, a nine-day celebration of the cocoa bean. It is also the venue of one of Europe's biggest and best festivals – the Umbria Jazz Festival – when world-famous artistes perform in the ancient piazzas in early July. It is also a city of great artists and sculptors.

The pedestrianized Corso Vannucci is named after Umbria's greatest painter, the 15th-century Pietro Vannucci known simply as Perugino, whose frescoes are masterpieces of the Italian Renaissance. The medieval Piazza IV Novembre runs off the Corso, where the centrepiece of the fountain-splashed piazza is the Fontana Maggiore. Created by medieval sculptors Nicola Pisano and son Giovanni, it is carved in elegant figures representing every theme from religious to pagan and mythical, including scenes from *Aesop's Fables*. Just to the north of the fountain are the steps to the Gothic cathedral San Lorenzo. Among the treasures therein are works by Perugino and what is said to be the Virgin's 'wedding ring' hewn out of agate. A *passeggiata* – where everyone strolls to see and be seen – along the northern end of the Corso leads to the huge Gothic Palazzo dei Priori, claimed by the Perugians as Italy's most beautiful public building.

BELOW *View across the rooftops of medieval Perugia, the capital of Umbria*

ABOVE *Marble statue on the exterior of the 13th-century Gothic Duomo San Lorenzo*

LEFT *The 13th-century graceful Fontana Maggiore, sculpted by Nicola and Giovanni Pisano in the central Piazza IV Novembre*

Spoleto

Beautifully sited on a hill guarding the fertile Vale of Spoleto, the poet Shelley was moved to call this 'the most romantic city I ever saw'. Nowadays it is also internationally famous for its Festival dei Due Mondi (Two Worlds' Festival), drawing together Europe and the Americas in a summer arts jamboree, founded by the Italian-American composer Giancarlo Menotti. The town's glory is epitomized in the Romanesque Duomo with its graceful façade, free-standing campanile built of Roman stone with exquisite 12th-century rose windows. Inside, in the apse, is the final fresco cycle by Fra Filippo Lippi begun in 1467. The vibrantly-coloured masterpieces portray scenes from *The Life of the Virgin* and the work was almost finished when the master died suddenly in 1469, to be finished by his assistants a few months later.

Most famous of all Spoleto's monuments, however, is the superb 14th-century aqueduct, the Ponte delle Torri. This 'bridge of towers' spans the yawning Tessino gorge, supported by 10 enormous arches up to a dizzying height of 262ft (80m) – an extraordinary feat of medieval engineering, designed by Gattapone from Gubbio. From here there are glorious views across the wooded countryside and to the Castelmonte mountains.

BELOW The white and gold interior of Duomo di Santa Maria Assunta, with Filippo Lippi's Life of the Virgin *fresco cycle in the background*

LEFT *The ceiling of Duomo di Santa Maria Assunta, with Filippo Lippi's* Life of the Virgin *fresco cycle covering the apse*

ABOVE *Exterior of Duomo di Santa Maria Assunta, showing its eight rose windows, Renaissance portico and 12th-century campanile*

Lazio & Abruzzo

Rome is Lazio's main destination, but the neighbouring countryside is where Romans have escaped to since ancient times. The province that surrounds Italy's capital has shimmering lakes, mountains and rolling countryside, dotted with olive trees and vineyards and crowned with hilltop villages, and archaeological sites.

Wealthy Romans have always loved their villas in the countryside and Tivoli, on the slopes of the Sabine Hills, was a favourite retreat. The theatrical water features of the Villa d'Este and the waterside remains of Hadrian's country retreat, Villa Adriana (the Roman Empire's former luxurious palace) testify that the beautiful gardens of Lazio were filled with fountains and mythological statuary to soothe and delight the soul.

Long before the Roman Empire was even a glimmer in the eye of Augustus, the northern part of this land was dominated by the proud Etruscans. Although cultured and very artistic, they left few traces of their lives but their deaths are recorded in the grassy tumulus tombs that are celebrations of life itself. Tarquinia was probably the capital of the Etruscans, whose glory now lies in its vivid tomb paintings.

Above ground, the remains of Rome's original main port at Ostia Antica, with its exquisite mosaics and architecture, are a fascinating insight into one of Italy's best-preserved Roman towns. On the northeastern side of Rome, Abruzzo stretches from the Apennine mountains to the Adriatic Sea. This rugged region has the highest mountains in Central Italy and vast tracts of ancient beech forests, where wolves and bears still roam.

Water feature and statuary at Villa Adriana, Tivoli, Lazio

Etruscan towns

Before the Romans, the northern part of Lazio was dominated by the Etruscan civilization. While the Etruscans left few traces of their lives, their deaths are recorded in famous burial grounds. Ancient Etruria was composed of 12 city states of which Tarquinia, founded in the 10th century BC, was the most important. Its glory today lies in its vivid tomb paintings, which seem to come alive with sacred or profane energy. 'A sense of the quick ripple of life… a quiet flow of touch' is how D H Lawrence described the tomb paintings of Tarquinia. Lawrence declared himself to be attracted instinctively to the Etruscans for their superb craftsmanship and voluptuous celebration of life. The maze of tombs at the Etruscan necropolis near the site of the ancient capital city is concealed by a grassy hilltop. The vibrantly coloured paintings mixed from lapis lazuli dust, charcoal and iron oxide depict athletic young men, lusty, feasting couples and the motifs of birds and dolphins. Thousands of tombs have been discovered and excavation continues to this day.

Nearby, the necropolis near Cerveteri, known as Banditaccia, contains thousands of tombs laid out in a city-like plan, with streets, grass-covered tumuli and tombs. This 'City of the Dead' depicts daily life in the frescoed tombs, many of which are replicas of Etruscan houses, in an extraordinarily moving testimony to this vanished culture. Painted in stucco, everyday items such as kitchen utensils and house pets represented their desire to place in their tombs everything that made life beautiful and desirable. The Etruscans believed in the cult of the afterlife and, as Lawrence says in *Etruscan Places*, 1932, a visit to their sites is curiously life-affirming: 'There is still a stillness and softness in these great grassy mounds with their ancient stone girdles, and down the central walk there lingers a kind of loneliness and happiness.'

BELOW *Exterior of a circular Etruscan barrow tomb within the necropolis, Cerveteri, on the site of an ancient Etruscan trading port*

RIGHT *The interior of an Etruscan barrow tomb in the necropolis at Cerveteri*

BELOW *The Tomb of the Augurs is probably the best-known Etruscan tomb in Tarquinia. Dating to about 530BC the frescoes depict Etruscan sport in the almost festival-like atmosphere of funerary games*

Gran Sasso d'Italia

Abruzzo is a sparsely populated, wild and mountainous region dotted with shepherds tending their flocks in time-honoured tradition. The eastern border is fringed by long, sandy beaches fronting the Adriatic, but to the west are the foothills of the Apennine mountains, which run the entire length of the country. The loftiest peak in the range, the Gran Sasso or 'Great Stone' towers at 9,560ft (2,914m) and is the centrepiece of the Parco Nazionale del Gran Sasso-Laga, which was established in 1993. This is the largest national park in Abruzzo, covering 994 square miles (1,600sq km) and is a glorious landscape of mountains, deep gorges, lakes, rivers and waterfalls. These are the highest mountains in continental Italy south of the Alps and the best region for mountaineering and skiing. The landscape is dotted with little towns and fortified medieval villages clinging to the mountain flanks which lend the area a feeling of wilderness. There is even a glacier in the park – Il Calderone (the cauldron), on the north face of the jagged vertical walls of Corno Grande – the only glacier in the Apennines and the farthest south in Europe. The capital of Abruzzo, the medieval mountain town L'Aquila (The Eagle), looks out from its eyrie on to the spectacular Gran Sasso massif.

OPPOSITE *The buildings of Tossica nestle in the hills of the Gran Sasso, backed by the snow-covered Gran Sasso ridge*

BELOW *A large, crumbling, old farmhouse perched on a steep hillside in the Gran Sasso – one of the largest massifs in the easternmost part of the central Apennines*

Villa d'Este

The Villa d'Este is a 16th-century pleasure palace with a sequence of fantastic fountains and water features in its shady grounds. Often referred to as the *Giardino delle Meravigli* (Garden of Miracles), it is included in the UNESCO World Heritage list and brings to mind one of the wonders of the ancient world, the hanging gardens of Babylon. These extraordinary gardens were created between 1560 and 1572 under the instruction of Cardinal Ippolito d'Este, the son of Lucrezia Borgia and Alfonso d'Este. They occupy a stretch of hillside below the town of Tivoli with fabulous views over the plain towards Rome. The villa itself was built around an earlier monastery and is lavishly decorated with frescoes and internal fountains, but the gardens are particularly striking – a terraced extravaganza of showstopping fountains. Cardinal d'Este wanted to create the most spectacular water garden ever seen, but at that time there was one great problem – a lack of water. He overcame this by ordering the diversion of the River Aniene via an aqueduct and underground tunnel to the top of the garden. Similarly great feats of engineering were the innumerable terraces which were gradually filled with water staircases, grottoes, fountains and water tricks. These mechanical wonders include the hydraulic Fontana dell'Organo (Organ Fountain) which plays tunes and trumpet blasts, and the Owl Fountain, which simulates birdsong – both of which have been recently renovated. Pyramids of water splash along the Viale delle Cento Fontane (Avenue of 100 Fountains), which traverses the middle of the gardens, pouring water into three channels, representing the main tributaries of the Tiber. These flow from the Oval Fountain (or the Fountain of Tivoli) at one end of the terrace towards the Rometta (Fountain of Rome) at the other, where the channels meet below a miniature version of the city. Other highlights include the Fountain of the Dragon and Fountain of Diana of Ephesus where water gushes from the goddess's countless breasts.

BELOW *The Fountain of Neptune near to the Fontana dell'Ovato at Villa d'Este ruins at Tivoli, just outside Rome*

LEFT *Villa d'Este's atmospheric Fontana dell'Ovato (Oval Fountain), also called Fontana di Tivoli (Tivoli Fountain), is backed by a nymphaeum peopled with basking marble nymphs by Giovanni Battista della Porta*

Villa Adriana

Emperor Hadrian's country retreat was the greatest imperial palace of the Roman Empire. Work started on it in AD 118, below the foothills of Tivoli, and Hadrian's aim was to re-create some of the wonders that he had seen on his extensive travels around the world. This great emperor was also a designer, poet and intellectual and his nickname 'Greekling' reflected his admiration for Greek culture. Although it is the most complete estate to have survived the fall of the Roman Empire, much of the original marble and travertine was removed from here to build the Villa d'Este nearby.

What is visible today among the remains is the most important Roman example of an Alexandrian garden. At its centre is the Canopus – a re-creation of the Egyptian town of Canope with its Temple of Serapis, near Alexandria. This long, rectangular canal, lined with Egyptian statues, represents a branch of the Nile. It also commemorates the place where Hadrian lost his beloved Antonius, a Greek boy who drowned in the river. In the Teatro Marittimo Hadrian would escape to contemplate in a little palace ringed by Iconic columns set in the middle of a circular lagoon. The extensive retreat also had very sophisticated *terme* (baths), theatres, Greek and Latin libraries and extensive housing for guests and staff, all set among the formal gardens adorned with statues, fountains and pools. Below ground he even built a fanciful re-creation of the underworld, Hades, reached through the *Cryptoportici* – a series of connecting subterranean passages. Covering an area of 180 acres (73 hectares), this was more of an imperial garden city than a villa and, in its heyday, was a huge open-air museum featuring the finest architecture of the Roman world. The villa fell into ruin after AD 700, when tribes of barbarians used it as a campsite. The artwork reappeared much later in private collections, and in various European museums as testament to the extraordinary life and times of Hadrian.

ABOVE *View of antique statuary along the Canopus at Villa Adriana, Tivoli, just outside Rome*

OPPOSITE *Cheeky statue at the Canopus, Villa Adriana*

Ostia Antica

Originally on the coast, the splendidly preserved remains of Ostia Antica are 20 miles (32km) from Rome. The place takes its name from the Latin *ostium*, meaning mouth, referring to its position at the mouth of the Tiber River. A mere fishing village in the 4th century BC, it went on to become the port of Ancient Rome for 600 years before its decline and silting up under sand and river mud. But it was those very deposits that protected the remains and today this is one of Italy's best-preserved Roman towns. The peaceful, grassy ruins sprawl over a vast area of 10,000 acres (4,047 hectares) of timeless beauty, interrupted only by the buzz of crickets in the trees.

The main street, Decumanus Maximus, still bears the imprint of ruts left by the four-wheeled carts used to ferry merchandise to and from Rome. The central square, Piazzale delle Corporazioni, was where corporations maintained trading links with the Roman world and remains of ancient offices, warehouses and shops still flank this square.

Much of the city is beautifully preserved with some of the finest mosaics and architecture from the ancient world. The Roman version of an apartment block is visible in the Casa di Diana, dating from the 2nd century AD, where four and five-storey buildings have an internal courtyard, just as their modern-day Italian counterparts have. The Baths of Neptune (Terme di Nettuno) have fine mosaics, including Neptune riding four horses through the sea and a cupid riding a dolphin. And, alongside the bath complex there is the Forica – a 24-person public lavatory, where the Romans would exchange gossip and do business.

ABOVE *Pillars in different stages of decay bounding paved roadway in the archaeological site of Ostia Antica, the port of Ancient Rome*

RIGHT *A surviving section of wall mosaic within the remains on the archaeological site of Ostia Antica*

LEFT *The beautifully preserved mosaic floors in the Baths of Neptune, Ostia Antica*

Parco Nazionale d'Abruzzo

Proudly known as the 'Region of Parks', one third of Abruzzo's territory is currently under environmental protection. A magnificent landscape of 154 sq.miles (400 sq. km) forms this region of snow-capped mountains, forests and undulating meadows. Established in 1922, this was Italy's first national park, created in an attempt to preserve part of the Apennine chain. The logo of Abruzzo is represented by the Marsican brown bear, which still roams here along with Apennine wolves. Once hunted to near extinction, these shy bears are still an endangered species but an estimated 100 live in the Park, while some 60 wolves prowl – announced by the occasional howl. It is also the perfect living environment for herds of chamois, red and roe deer and rarer species such as otters, wildcats and Apennine lynx and pine martens. There are about 300 different varieties of resident birds in the park and, during spring and summer, the meadows, valleys and woodlands are carpeted by beautiful wildflowers including two endemic species – the Marsican iris and lady's-slipper. And on the higher reaches alpine flora, including gentians and edelweiss, thrive.

Only one road crosses the park, but there are over 150 different walking routes and many cycling tracks. The area is perfect terrain too for horse riding and pony trekking.

OPPOSITE *A pony grazing in the winter sun among the stubbly grass in Abruzzo National Park*

LEFT *Brown bears still roam the forests of Abruzzo National Park*

BELOW *A river flowing from snow-covered mountains through the sparsely wooded lowlands of Abruzzo National Park*

HOTEL MARINA

Campania

Along the 'shinbone' and towards the 'upper foot' of the boot-shaped Italian peninsula there is a beautiful land that seems untouched by the present but by every other era of its country's history — going back over two-and-a-half millennia. Campania encompasses Naples and the fertile region between the Tyrrhenian coast of southern Italy and the western slopes of the Apennines.

Since the 6th century BC, when the Greeks arrived and built their temples, through the arrival of the Etruscans and the eventual supremacy of the Romans, the region has been victim to colonization, foreign invasion, domination and neglect — by Normans, Angevin French, Germans and Spanish. The tragedy of Campania's neglect continued well into the 20th century, when it remained a backwater of the modern, unified Italy. It was only when the outside world sought access to the region that its tragedy turned into triumph. Incomers discovered the glorious resorts of the Amalfi coast, the museums of historic Naples, the Greek temple of Paestum, the ruins of Pompeii and the volcanic Mount Vesuvius, whose eruption destroyed and simultaneously preserved an entire Roman town as its people went about their daily lives.

Emerging from an almost feudal world, today Campania most of all enlightens visitors to the fact that there was an Italy beyond Rome, Florence, Venice, Genoa and other northern cities. An easy-going Italy where old values survived, where old rituals are still observed and enacted, where the world once stood still.

Symbol of a new dawn, the Amalfi coast basks in sunlight while menacingly bleak mountains recall a dramatic past

ABOVE *The view from Amalfi along the Costiera Amalfitana, where the whitewashed houses of neighbouring villages spill down the mountains to the azure sea below*

Amalfi

The country of Italy may not have been created by the mythological wolves that gave birth to the twin founders of Rome, nor even by great emperors who came to rule it. Maybe it was, as one writer suggested, 'born of a landscape created by the paintbrush of God and nurtured and decorated by ordinary people over thousands of years'. If this were so, then the real Italy would be Amalfi.

Its 30-mile (50-km) coastline, *Costiera Amalfitana* has been described as the most beautiful in the Mediterranean. It also belongs to neighbouring Sorrento, Positano and Salerno — but takes Amalfi's name because of the town's important historical role in the region when it was Italy's oldest republic, founded in 840. In the 11th century it became a great maritime power and laid down the *Tavole Amalfitane* (Amalfi Navigation Tables), the world's oldest maritime code.

Part of the modern attraction of the town is its proximity to its coastal neighbours and hillside towns, and it's a good base from which to visit Naples, Pompeii, Herculaneum and Mount Vesuvius.

Amalfi is famous for its highly attractive setting. The focus of the town's ancient heritage is the 10th-century Duomo di Sant'Andrea, perched imposingly at the top of radiating flights of stairs, and its great bronze doors, which were cast in Constantinople around 1066. Alongside is the Chiostro del Paradiso, a magical Moorish-style cloister, like a vision of paradise, blending Romanesque and Arab styles. But the highlight for most is the scenic drive along the corniche that winds along this spectacular coastline, where the ciffs plunge precipitously into the deep blue sea.

LEFT *Dining out in Amalfi is a delight because of the wide selection of eateries available. They all tend to have their own specialities but these often involve some mouthwatering form of mixed seafood antipasti*

Pompeii

We had scarcely sat down to rest when darkness fell, not the dark of a moonless or cloudy night, but as if the lamp had been put out in a closed room… You could hear the shrieks of women, the wailing of infants and the shouting of men; some were calling their parents, others their children or their wives, trying to recognize them by their voices. People bewailed their own fate or that of their relatives, and there were some who prayed for death in their terror of dying. Many besought the aid of the gods, but still more imagined there were no gods left, and that the Universe was plunged into eternal darkness for evermore.

Above is the eyewitness account of the 18-year-old Roman scholar Pliny the Younger of the catastrophe on 24 August, AD 79, when Mount Vesuvius erupted in a fury of flames and sulphur wiping out Pompeii.

RIGHT *The statue of a dancing fawn unearthed from the Casa del Fauno (House of the Faun), the largest and one of the most opulent houses excavated during the recovery of Pompeii*

BELOW *A Roman version of the Birth of Venus, showing the goddess emerging from an oyster shell, was one of the frescoes found in a home now known as the 'House of Venus'*

Out of the ashes…

The young Pliny survived and went on to become a writer of some note, but thousands, including his uncle, died under the volcanic ashes that buried an entire city of some 20,000. But the apocalyptic tragedy of Pompeii had paradoxically created an archaeological miracle in another time-zone. Although the city – a settlement about 12 miles (20km) to the southwest of Naples – remained lost and forgotten for over 1,500 years, it was eventually discovered by accident and excavations were later begun in 1748. What has been uncovered so far (the work continues to a lesser extent) is a vast three-dimensional, tactile snapshot of a day in the life of a Roman community, all largely intact thanks to the preservative properties of the volcanic ash. The examples of art and architecture that survived are remarkable enough, but far more moving are the remains and reconstructions of everyday life in the midst of death. There are exact reproductions of figures as they appeared at the moment of death. These were created by pouring plaster into the holes formed by the volcanic liquid that enveloped the bodies, then setting them into solid 'casts'. There are visible recreations of the worlds of commerce and manual labour, and of lives that were lived in homes, large and small. Outside the House of the Tragic Poet there is a mosaic of a dog and the words *Cave Canem* (Beware of the Dog). There are temples, a forum, baths, fountains, pavements, street signs, a vast amphitheatre, private houses, shops, a necropolis – even a bordello with explicit menus and paintings on the wall – and gardens that were recreated using the seeds found in the soil.

ABOVE *A fresco of a warrior standing ready for battle with s hield, spear, cloak – and very little else – was found in one of the Pompeii buildings*

LEFT *Structures like this colonnade from a Pompeii public building helped archaeologists and historians piece together the sort of society that had evolved in this Roman city*

Capri

Capri is perhaps the best known of the islands of the Bay of Naples. Measuring only just over 6 square miles (10 square km), this pleasure island has glorious views from almost every corner. It was once the hedonistic home of the Emperor Tiberius back in AD 27 whose Villa Jovis (the Residence of Jupiter, the fabled 'bringer of joy') brought a great deal of joy to the emperor – but sometimes in rather perverted style, according to the ancient scribes who catalogued some lewd activities. Many visitors to this 'Island of Goats' – which is where the name *Capri* comes from – detect a certain old-fashioned charm. Countless 20th-century icons such as entertainer Gracie Fields and writer Oscar Wilde were passionately in love with the isle, but it is enjoying a renaissance this century with ultra-luxurious spa hotels catering to the *fashionista* set's every whim and a burgeoning set of celebrities in hideaway villas in the exclusive Anacapri. Capri town is perennially popular: the main square, called the *Piazetta*, is like a stage set and the perfect place to sit at sundown with a *limoncello*, a delicious potent liquor made from lemons. Gorgeous boutiques and cafés cluster around the domed church of Santo Stefano and, in the distance, tiny coves beckon, set against a backdrop of citrus, fig and olive trees and scented wild flowers. Along the coast is the *Grotta Azzura* (Blue Grotto), a hidden cave that is startlingly suffused with amazing sapphire-blue light.

OPPOSITE *Faraglioni is the collective name for the three spectacular rocky islets, or 'sirens', on the Capri coast. Their individual names (from left) are Stella, Mezzo and Scopolo*

BELOW *The expansive ruins of the Villa Jovis, on a promontory facing the mainland. It was the home of the Emperor Tiberius, after he retired there in AD 27*

Naples

PAGE 127 *Easter Festival in the Quartieri Spagnoli (Spanish Quarter) – one of the city's 12 annual festivals, which are public holidays, when the celebrations spill colourfully and wildly out of the churches and into the streets*

BELOW *The 16th-century Castel Nuovo gets its name from the legend that the poet Virgil buried an egg (uovo) on this site, predicting that its breakage would herald some disaster*

A legend from Homer that says that when Odysseus escaped the sweet but deadly lure of the siren's call by binding himself to the ship's mast, the siren Parthenope became so frustrated that she drowned herself in the Bay of Naples. The name 'Naples' derives from the Greek *Neapolis*, meaning 'New City'. And so it was, back in 650-600 BC, when it was founded by settlers from Greece.

Many have found inspiration in the Bay of Naples, under the menacing presence of Mount Vesuvius, a fact that illustrates the contrast between the terrible and the sublime. The city's chaotic traffic, hanging washing, peeling buildings and petty criminals are all much in evidence. But so, too, are superb buildings, outstanding museums, bustling markets, beautiful people strutting on a continual stage set and gusty, voluptuous delights in a city that also gave us the authentic pizza.

The Museo Nazionale Archeologicco, has one of the finest collections of frescoes and mosaics in Europe, together with the Farnese Bull – the largest classical sculpture ever found – and many of the best finds from Pompeii, including the 'secret cabinet'of erotic art.

For other forms of entertainment, the opera house, Teatro San Carlo, is Italy's largest and oldest. But excitement lurks around every corner. In the area known as the Quartieri Spagnoli, the narrowest of streets are hung with washing and colourful characters chat, gesticulate and put the world to rights, in the stereotypical image of the passionate and exuberant city that is Naples.

Treasures of the Amalfi Coast

The town of Amalfi itself, with its distinctive cathedral, and its colourfully neat buildings and houses scaling the cliffs and the lower reaches of the rugged mountains that seemingly cuddle the town – is a delight to behold. And it is richly deserving of the epithet conferred on the whole of the Costiera Amalfitana – which includes Sorrento, Positano and Salerno – as the most beautiful coastline in the Mediterranean.

In close-up, Amalfi is a warm and comfortable town that has accepted with grace its decline as a once-great capital of a powerful republic which grew rich on mercantile trade and banking. But there is still a hint of grandeur – not least in the marvellously ornate Duomo, the Cathedral of Saint Andrew, where some of the fisherman apostle's remains are preserved. The building is reached via a flight of 57 steps to the atrium, which leads into the elegant Chiostra del Paradiso (Paradise Cloister), a Moorish structure originally built in 1268, which is often the setting for concerts by singers and musicians. This in turn leads to the crypt where the saint's tomb is kept, along with a golden reliquary, which is used to carry the saint's bones during processions on holy days.

If you sense a citric tang in the air while wandering around the town, it may not just be from the fruit stalls and shops – the area around this coast is famous for its lemons. In fact the Amalfi lemon, called the 'queen' of lemons, is a very particular variety grown on rocky terraces clinging to the hillsides. They've been around for quite a while – they are depicted in 1st-century frescoes which were found in the houses of Pompeii.

Amalfi is also famous for its earthenware products. The town has a long tradition of ceramics, reflecting the stylish Italian love of pottery, and Amalfi goods are sold all over the world. Incidentally, if you want to make your own you can learn – Amalfi style – at pottery classes that are given in nearby Minori.

OVERLEAF *The atrium and the Moorish-style Paradise Cloisters of the Duomo di Sant'Andrea, where some of the saint's relics are kept*

INSIDE *A view from the sea of Amalfi, a cosy town that was once capital of a great mercantile republic embracing the entire coastal region*

BELOW *A pottery shop in the town. Amalfi has a long and strong tradition in local ceramics and boldly designed pottery*

HOTEL
CENTRALE
ALBERGO
S. ANDREA

WALTER!

HOTEL RESIDENCE

LEFT *Local citrus growers use special techniques to grow the Amalfi lemon, which is available in shops throughout the town*

MARIA
VATTIENTE
DE
QUARTIERI
SPAGNOLI
VICO CANALE
N°17

Paestum

Some of the stumps of stones, bricks and columns that are visible in the pictures on these pages are actually older than the Parthenon of Athens. The large building is considered by many to be the finest Doric temple of all time. And yet this is not Greece: these ruins have been part of the landscape of southern Italy for well over two-and-a-half thousand years.

Near Salerno, to the southeast of Naples, the site of Paestum has three Greek temples which are among the remnants of a 6th-century BC Greek city – a community with an *agora* (market place), forum, gymnasium and seat of government. Legend says it was founded by Jason and the Argonauts, but historians are not entirely convinced.

Poseidonia (Land of Neptune), as it was known before the Romans came, has survived in the distinctive forms of three temples – the Temple of Neptune, the Temple of Hera and the Temple of Ceres.

The Temple of Neptune, which takes its name from the Roman version of the original name of the settlement, is the largest and is extremely well preserved. The Temple of Hera (Juno), the oldest, is named after the wife of Jupiter, the goddess of marriage and women. The Temple of Ceres (Demeter), named after the goddess of tillage and soil, was built much later but survived being a ruin and became a church in the Middle Ages. Together they are an awe-inspiring spectacle. Seeing them you might agree with the 19th-century English writer George Eliot that the site is 'the finest thing, I verily believe, we have seen in Italy'.

ABOVE *Visiting sightseers are dwarfed by the hugeness of the columns of the Greek temples at Paestum, near Salerno, in Campania*

LEFT *The Temple of Neptune, in its full glory. This Greek cathedral dedicated to the God of the Sea in a city once called Poseidonia, is the most spectacular on the site*

Ravello

The view from the hill above the Villa Rufolo in Ravello is among the most beautiful in the whole of the region. It is a sight that has been beheld and beloved by many notable people, including a number of great artists who chose to make their home here – among them the composers Richard Wagner and Franz Liszt, and writer Virginia Woolf and most of the Bloomsbury set, and in more recent times the controversial American writer Gore Vidal. There may be something creative in the air here because two of the greatest literary works of the 20th century – D H Lawrence's *Lady Chatterley's Lover* and Graham Greene's *The Third Man* – were written while the authors were staying at Villa Rufolo. The garden villa, a 14th-century manor house built in Ravello's heyday as a merchant town, fell into decay when the town's fortunes declined. It was bought by a visiting Scotsman in 1851 and restored to its past and present twin-cloistered glory as a masterpiece of Sicilian-Moorish design.

Ravello's other garden estate, Villa Cimbrone, has a less authentic pedigree, having been put together using ancient bits and pieces by a British aristocrat about 100 years ago. Even so, it is a magnificent piece of design and the view from the belvedere rivals that of Villa Rufolo.

Some writers have described Ravello as a Pompeii-style time capsule. Because of the suddenness of the town's economic decline, much of the town remains exactly as it was when the bankers and merchants fled, and therefore some quite anonymous streets and buildings are snapshots of 14th-century Campania. But the beautiful old villas, the palazzi, cobbled pathways and romantic gardens make this, one of Italy's most photogenic and photographed spots, eternally loved and idyllic.

ABOVE *The splendidly restored gardens and grounds of the 14th-century, twin-cloistered Villa Rufolo afford glorious views over the Amalfi coast*

OPPOSITE *The view of Ravello from the sea. The town sits upon the most dramatically rugged coastline of Campania, with terraces like stepping stones up the cliff-face*

MONTIS

The Deep South

The great 18th-century freedom fighter, Giuseppe Garibaldi, gave the name *Il Mezzogiorno*, the land of the midday sun, to the whole of Italy south of Rome; a sun-drenched land of dramatic contrasts where the newly rich and achingly poor, the majestic and barren, ornate and humble all exist amid glorious, untamed landscapes.

The 'toe' of the boot-shaped Italian peninsula belongs to the regions of Basilicata and Calabria. Sparsely populated, remote and rugged, this has always been an area where bandits have taken cover, but it is also littered with Greek remains, castles, abbeys and fascinating cities. Matera, the UNESCO World Heritage Site, is an extraordinary example of ancient and modern where people lived literally in *'sassi'*, caves, until quite recently.

Puglia, the 'heel' of the Italian 'boot', has the longest coastline of any region in Italy. The forested and mountainous Gargano peninsula plunges to the turquoise seas, while the inland plains have their own treasures from imposing castles such as Castel del Monte to the humble *trulli* around Alberobello. These fairytale little conical dwellings resembling hobbit houses have mysterious origins and even magical significance. Farther south, at the tip of the 'heel' is the 'Florence of the South', where Lecce, known for its exuberantly voluptuous architecture, is referred to as 'Lecce baroque'. The white medieval towns, such as Ostuni, are dazzling against the rich red soil and carpets of silvery green olive groves and vineyards in this fertile region that produces most of Italy's olive oil and full-bodied wines.

Ostuni, the 'White Town', stands on three hills at the edge of the Murgia dei Trulli, near Alberobello (Puglia), its whitewashed buildings in dazzling contrast with the lush surrounding green valleys

Castel del Monte

Standing proud and solitary on the summit of a rock, Castel del Monte surveys the vast plains of Puglia. It is a masterpiece of medieval military architecture built by Frederick II of Hohenstaufen, Holy Roman Emperor and King of Sicily in the 1240s. Much later, in 1847, the landscape painter and poet Edward Lear wrote in his *Journals* that it was worth five hours of riding through 'dismal, shrubless' country, unrelieved by any 'distant prospect' to sketch this 'hunting palace'. Whether it was erected originally as a military outpost or as a hunting lodge – Frederick was a keen and very accomplished falconer – is still a matter of debate. What is undeniable, however, is that it is a harmonious and sympathetic synthesis of styles from classical antiquity, North European Gothic and the Near East, much of which was influenced by Sicily and its invaders. This blending of cultures reflects Frederick's multi-faceted personality. To his contemporaries he was known as *stupor mundi et immutator mirabilis* (wonder of the world and extraordinary innovator). Although Castel del Monte was only one of around 200 of his fortresses in southern Italy and Sicily, it was the only one that was not rectangular. The perfectly regular octagonal form is reflected in eight rooms on each floor and eight octagonal towers. The reasons Frederick may have had for the mathematical and astronomical precision of the octagonal layout remain shrouded in mystery. Reminders of the Romanesque past can be seen in the lions protruding from the gateway, while classical influences are still visible in the friezes and cornices, and the remains of the floor mosaic in the eighth room on the ground floor are seen to be distinctly Muslim in their influence. The castle is a UNESCO World Heritage Site and such is its fame that it even appears on the obverse side of the Italian euro one cent coin.

OPPOSITE *Federick II's Fortress the Castel del Monte's courtyard blending romanesque, Gothic, Classical and Muslim influences*

LEFT *View of the Castel del Monte dominating the plains near Ruvo di Puglia in the province of Bari*

Il Gargano

Known as the 'spur' of the elegant Italian 'boot', the Gargano peninsula is in the north of Puglia, straddling the sea and plains. It is a place of dark ancient forests, fishing villages, coastal watchtowers, shrines, caves and long, sandy beaches. Most of this mountainous promontory jutting into the Adriatic Sea is a National Park – the Parco Nazionale del Gargano, created in 1991. It is clothed with coastal forests of pine and ilex and orchards where almonds, oranges and olives grow. The majestic Foresta Umbra is at the heart of the Gargano National Park, where thick woods of beech, pine, wood and oak are silhouetted against the sky, in some places so dense that the sunlight cannot penetrate. This ancient forest was praised by writers such as Horace, one of the greatest Roman lyric poets (65-8 BC), who wrote of the magnificent oaks here. Today, the Umbra Forest is Italy's largest natural wooded area, rich in wildlife and fauna, including 65 types of orchid. Elsewhere on the Gargano peninsula is the vast Tavoliere plain, covering about 50 sq. miles (80 sq. km) where durum wheat, the main ingredient of the dark, tasty Apulian bread, is grown. Like a panoramic balcony overlooking the Tavoliere, the town of Monte Sant'Angelo is full of alleyways and stairways, with an imposing Norman castle at the top and old town centre enclosed by walls. Other walls surround the beautiful Manfredonia Castle, overlooking the sea, which houses the Gargano National Museum with its fascinating collection of Daunian steles, which are carved limestone slabs from the 6th-7th centuries BC. Set like pearls in this luxuriant vegetation are towns like Vieste, with winding alleyways and white houses, overhanging the sea, and Peschici, perched on a rocky promontory. And miles of long stretches of golden, sandy beaches dot the coastline. In Horace's words, *carpe diem* – seize the moment.

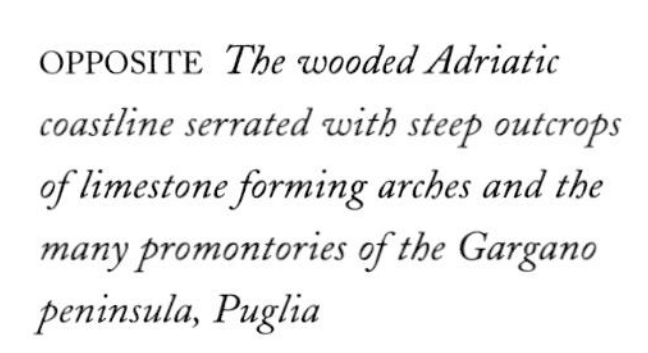

OPPOSITE *The wooded Adriatic coastline serrated with steep outcrops of limestone forming arches and the many promontories of the Gargano peninsula, Puglia*

RIGHT *Basilica di Santa Croce – the superb example of Lecce baroque with detailed relief stonework surrounding Lo Zingarello's rose window full of such splendid decorations as ornate and intricate as any the world has seen*

OPPOSITE *Altar of San Francesco di Paola worked in bas-relief by Antonio Zimbalo (1614-15) in the Santa Croce church*

Lecce

The exuberance of Lecce's architecture, which has earned this city the title 'Florence of the South', is due to the local yellow pinkish-tinged stone. Its malleability and the great skill of craftsmen have etched out this lovely city's proud boast as one of the most unified urban landscapes in Italy.

Lecce existed in Greek times during the Trojan War and was later conquered by the Romans and became an important centre of the Roman Empire. A well-preserved Roman amphitheatre (2nd century AD) dominates the southern half of the main piazza, the cobblestoned Piazza Sant'Oronzo. But for the gloriously ornate and intricate *Barocco leccese* 'Lecce baroque' for which this city is so famous, the most perfect example is the Basilica della Santa Croce. Cherubs, grotesque human shapes, flowers, fruits and fantasy allegorical animals are the beauties and beasts that adorn the basilica. Begun in 1549, it took 150 years to complete, with the upper part of the façade largely attributed to Giuseppe Zimbalo, nicknamed *Lo Zingarello* (the Gipsy) in the 17th century. Together with his brother, Antonio, he created most of the masterpieces of Lecce in the middle years of the 17th century. The interior is serene and uplifting where the naves soar to a great height and the large altar has scenes from the life of San Francesco da Paola worked in bas-relief by Antonio Zimbalo (1614-15). While Baroque architecture generally is overblown, the Lecce version is certainly exuberant and dazzlingly ornate, but at the same time refined. The stone, with its warm golden hue, is soft and easy to carve into complex, intricate shapes. Later, it hardens as it ages, thus miraculously preserving the mason's craftsmanship for our enjoyment. The city has more than 40 churches and at least as many noble palaces that were built or renovated here between the middle of the 17th century and the end of the 18th. Swirling columns, fantastic figures, ornate altars and curving yellow palaces are the trademarks of this glorious city, which at every corner dazzles with its beauty.

CORONA IVSTITIAE
FLORENTI
SICVT LILIVM
CHA
RI
TAS

Alberobello

They stand in rows like little beehives reaching towards azure skies, with pinnacles of crosses and strange stone markers that are said to have magical significance. The lush Istria Valley, a UNESCO World Heritage Site, has these unique 'hobbit' houses, scattered in picturesque disorder throughout the countryside. The dry stone 'trulli' homes have made Alberobello their capital, the hilltop setting of this fairytale town in sun-drenched Puglia. Alberobello (meaning oak wood) began as a farming village near an oak wood, growing up around a 6th-century abbey; in 1797 it was raised to the rank of city by the King of Naples. The southern part of the village is the 'trulli district', of which there are well over a thousand – in groups and standing along the steep, winding streets that climb up the hill. The white luminosity from these fabled little dwellings bounces back from every angle and curve. The heat disappears as if by magic on crossing the thresholds, where thick walls ingeniously protect from both cool winters and sizzling hot summers. At one time seven or eight people would have lived in these tiny homes, the children upstairs and the horse with his manger and the adults below. Nowadays, many have been restored to make bijou homes and artists' workshops and others extended to become hotels. The emblems with which so many are tattooed represent Christianity, with its crosses and speared hearts, as well as primitive and pagan times with symbols of Saturn, the god of agriculture and the winged god, Mercury. The trulli take their name from the Greek *tholos* (cupola) and were made out of the local calcerous stone without any binding mortar. Some say they can be traced to the end of the 9th century, when Puglia came under Byzantine rule, another theory is that they were a tax dodge – a notorious Italian pastime – as they could be classified as 'unfinished'. Whatever their origins, these *trulli* are unique.

RIGHT *Trulli, the unique beehive-shaped dwellings, huddle together in the narrow streets of Alberobello, the trulli capital, in Puglia*

VENIRS DA MARCO
VINI E OLIO
LOCALE

Matera

In the last century, the battered landscape of the earthquake-riven deforested province of Basilicata became known through Carlo Levi's book *Christ Stopped at Eboli* (*Cristo si è Fermato a Eboli*). In this book he talks of the treeless slopes 'eroded into a pattern of holes and hillocks, like a landscape of the moon'. And yet, although Basilicata may be southern Italy's poorest region, it is also the most underdeveloped, with glorious tracts of unspoilt countryside and historic treasures. It also has a small but beautiful coastline, where the area around Maratea rivals the Amalfi coast for its sheer and unblemished loveliness. Inland, southern Italy's hidden treasure, Matera – not to be confused with Maratea – is in the heart of 'I sassi' – literally meaning 'the stones', which are extraordinary cave-dwellings, hewn into rock and stacked one on top of another. This remarkable town, perched over a deep ravine, is a UNESCO World Heritage Site and has played an important part in the film industry, including a location for Mel Gibson's *The Passion of the Christ*. Originally built in Byzantine times as churches, the *sassi* were used until relatively recently by the inhabitants as dwellings. These windowless caves had damp walls and earthen floors, where the whole family including the animals would sleep side by side. Eventually façades and roofs were added and nearly 15,000 people were still living in them in 1952, when the government finally declared them unhealthy and outlawed their use. Carlo Levi likened the living conditions to Dante's *Inferno* during his exile to the area in the 1930s. But this is the most outstanding, intact example of a troglodyte settlement in the Mediterranean region, believed to be one of the oldest communities in the world. And from those stones there are new beginnings. Several of the *sassi* have been transformed into bijou hotels — fascinating, spacious and hugely atmospheric, set in a stunning location.

LEFT *Sasso Barisano quarter and cathedral in Matera – one of the two sassi (cave) districts – the other being the Sasso Caveoso*

REBECCA·VADIT·CV·SERVO·ABRAHE
REBECCA
EVA
ADAM

Sicily & Sardinia

Sicily and Sardinia are, in that order, Italy's largest islands and have individual characters which set them apart from the mainland by more than the sea. Sicily, with a population of five million and covering 10,000 sq. miles (26,000 sq.km), is the largest island in the Med, with Sardinia the next largest with a population of about 1.7 million and an area of 9,300 sq.m (24,000 sq.km).

Historically, Sicily is a cradle of civilization in its own right and is very much shaped by its own past as well as by the earth-moving influences of Europe's largest active volcano, Mount Etna. The fiery dragon not only distinguishes the landscape, but also permeates the fragrance of the scents of the island – the flowers, pomegranates and lemons. This is especially true of the town of Taormina, which is a charming medieval settlement of narrow streets, elegant churches and lots of pleasant bars and cafés. Some distance away to the west, along the southern coast, the town of Agrigento is the focus of a great many stunning ruins which was, in the words of an eminent Greek writer, 'the most beautiful city of mortals'. Farther west, on the northern coast around the 12th-century city of Palermo, is one of the island's most spectacular cathedrals at Monreale.

Sardinia is more isolated than Sicily – and sufficiently different from the mainland to make it a favourite holiday destination for the Italians themselves. It's an island of colourful festivals. The most notable of these, the Festa de Sant'Efisio, takes place around the island's fascinating capital of Cágliari.

The cathedral at Monreale, near Palermo, whose elaborately intricate mosaic-work is rated among the best in the world

ABOVE *Sometimes referred to as the 'Michelin Man', the 26ft (8m) fallen telamon at the Temple of Jupiter (or Zeus) at Agrigento's magnificent Valley of the Temples*

RIGHT *The remarkably preserved sunlit ruins of the Temple of Concord is the best example of sacred Greek architecture to be found outside mainland Greece*

Agrigento

According to the Ancient Greeks, only Paradise could surpass the beauty of the city from which Agrigento grew. As it is today, it is a moderately interesting town with a medieval heart worth looking around. It has a number of attractive churches, a massive Duomo and a main street with quality jewellers, bookshops, boutiques and *pasticcerie*. But these are mere diversions compared to what Agrigento has to offer on its outskirts. The Valle dei Templi (Valley of the Temples) is what remains of the original, the Greek city founded in 581 BC, called Akragas, which historians have compared with Athens. It was a great and powerful city, which over the centuries suffered conquest and sacking by Carthaginians, Romans, Saracens and Normans. Even with its treasures plundered, what remains today is one of the most impressive collections of ruins outside Greece. Early in the year up to March and late in the year from October, most buildings on the site are illuminated and the effect is more dramatic than any Hollywood epic.

Among the ruins, the best-preserved is the Tempio della Concordia (Concord Temple), and only in Greece would you see anything more pristine. It dates back to around 430 BC, and owes its remarkable preservation in part because it was later taken over as a Christian church.

The Tempio di Giove (Jove, Jupiter or Zeus) is less well preserved, largely because it was never completed and was left to ruin by the Carthaginians. Even so, it is the largest Doric temple ever discovered. And one of the curiosities of the site is the 26ft (8m) long toppled column, sometimes called the 'Michelin Man' because it's composed of rounded 'tyres' of stone. In fact it is a *telamon* — a support column from the temple carved into the shape of a man.

What remains of the Tempio dei Dioscuri (Castor and Pollux) is actually a reconstructed hotchpotch of materials from the site. But, viewed against the backcloth of the modern suburbs of Agrigento, it's a jolting reminder of the venerability of the whole of the Valle dei Templi.

OPPOSITE *Looking north from the Valle dei Templi in the direction of Agrigento's sprawling suburbs, the Tempio del Dioscuri stands as a memorial to a glorious past*

Palermo

Unmistakably the capital of Sicily, Palermo's style is a compendium of influences from all parts and ages of the known world. Perched on the northwestern coast of the island, it is a sprawling, chaotic city with occasional moments of neatness and tranquillity. Oddly enough, these moments can occur in the city centre, which is marked by a crossroads and is officially called Piazza Vigliena – though it is better known as Quattro Canti (the Four Corners). It divides Palermo into four quadrants, each of which once had their own dialects, loyalties and palaces.

Just along from the Four Corners, going roughly eastwards, is the splendid Piazza Pretoria, which has an immense Baroque fountain populated by glistening white nudes in their fullest possible glory. It's said that the fountain – which is fenced off to deter excitable vandals – was originally built for a villa in northern Italy but never used. The city cathedral is equally central in the other direction from the Four Corners. It is a 12th-century building – constructed at the behest of Palermo's then archbishop, a certain Anglo-Norman known as 'Walter of the Mill' (*Gualtiero Offamiglio*) – which has undergone many restorations and changes up to the 18th century. Even so, it has retained some of its original good-looks, especially the east side where the original pair of towers flank an elaborate portico.

Palermo is alive with bustling markets. The most famous, the colourful Vucciria, is something of a microcosm of the city's Arabic past in lively casbah style, but there are many others. The markets at Piazza Ballaró and the adjoining Piazza del Cármine are a symphony of vendors' cries, a riot of colour and an array of exotic vegetables of all shapes and sizes.

BELOW *Although frequently renovated and restored in different styles, Palermo's cathedral has retained its original 12th-century twin towers, which now flank the portico*

ABOVE *Fruit and vegetables in all shapes, sizes and colours at the daily market at Palermo's Piazza Ballaró and Piazza del Cármine*

LEFT *Just one of the gleaming white nude statues that decorate the 16th-century Piazza Pretoria fountain, once destined for a rich man's villa in northern Italy*

Taormina

It's like living with a grumpy old man, still smoking, still grumbling and somewhat menacing. For the people of Taormina, having Mount Etna on their doorstep makes life interesting — as it did for the Ancient Greeks, who once thought Etna to be the kingdom of Vulcan, god of fire. Over 10,000ft (3,040m) high, it continues to smoke, cough, gurgle and comes out in a full-scale eruption periodically. The last big blast was in 2001, although there have been lesser eruptions as recently as September 2007.

Taormina, sitting on top of Mount Tauro and overlooking two beautiful Sicilian bays, is a small town with big charm full of fascinating medieval streets, elegant churches, and a great many bars and restaurants which cater for the visitors who come flocking here. The town basks in its dramatic proximity to the volcano and does a roaring tourist trade, attracting those who want to get a whiff of the grumbling giant from a comfortable distance or embark on one of the excursions to climb Etna when it is safe to do so. The town's tourist status has evolved largely because of the volcano. Previously it was just another hilltown on the northern Ionian coast of Sicily, distinguished by another piece of drama – as the home of a very fine Ancient Greek theatre. *Teatro Greco*, which rates as one of the best monuments in the whole of Italy, was constructed in 300 BC and maintained during Roman times, when it was the scene of gladiatorial contests. These days it stages quality drama and concerts while providing great views of Mount Etna and the Med.

The town also has some architectural gems celebrating styles of the 15th and 16th centuries at Palazzo Corvaja, which is also the location of a museum of Sicilian art and popular culture. The town's cathedral, *Cattedrale di San Nicola*, is a 13th-century building with battlements, but, more interestingly, the town also has a Roman version of the Teatro Greco, which was discovered in the 19th century and is today in use for public events. Art enthusiasts can get their fix at the Palazzo Duchi San Stefano, a Gothic building with Moorish and Norman influences, where there is a permanent sculpture exhibition.

Cultural attractions apart, Taormina also enjoys quite a social life. The *passeggiata* – that oh-so-Italian tradition of an early evening walk where everyone preens to see and be seen – is conducted with real enthusiasm and style.

OPPOSITE *Part of the impressive remains of Taormina's 3rd-century BC Greek Theatre (Teatro Greco) which has won this Sicilian hill-town the avid attention of the whole world*

BELOW *The mouth of the volcano. Still smoking, still grumbling, Mount Etna is an ever-present backcloth to life in the lovely, lively Sicilian town of Taormina*

TOP *Dressed up for the occasion, horses play a part in many of the festivals throughout Sardinia*

ABOVE *Headdresses are an important part of feminine attire on carnival day in Cagliari*

RIGHT *A colourful Sardinian beauty in full carnival costume for the Sagra di Sant'Efisio, which celebrates the martyrdom of a much-loved local saint at nearby Pula*

Sardinia Festival

Anyone visiting Sardinia for a week or more is bound to experience the joy of a carnival. The island is alive with colour, shrill music, dancing, feasting and sometimes fireworks on some 40 occasions throughout the year. Often the carnivals have a religious connection, but not always. Some pay homage to significant historical dates; some mark the harvest and others celebrate the advent of seasonal foods. Occasionally there's wild, uninhibited behaviour, but mainly they are good, clean fun.

Called *feste* or *sagri*, the biggest of them all is based in the island's capital of Cagliari. The *Sagra di Sant'Efisio* is a Maytime celebration of the martyrdom of the Sardinian saint – a 3rd-century Roman soldier who was put to death after converting to Christianity and whose spirit is credited with ending a 17th-century plague on the island. During the Mayday procession an effigy of Efisio is carried on a cart drawn by decorated oxen from the capital to the saint's church, some distance south at Nora, near Pula. It returns on the night of 4 May escorted by throngs of townsfolk, some on horseback, dressed in beautiful national costume. All this is accompanied by the shrill tones of the *launeddas* – a musical instrument composed of three reed pipes, two five-holed chanters and one drone. Unique to Sardinia, this 'triple clarinet' makes an appearance at many island festivals.

There isn't a month in the year when Sardinia is without a festival. After the Maytime celebrations, the festivals become more frequent with up to four a month during the summer and early autumn. Sardinia's second city, Sassari, has two major festivals – one at the end of May, which celebrates an AD 1000 victory over the Saracens and includes a spectacular horse race, and one in August called *I Candelieri* (The Candlesticks), featuring giant wooden candleholders paraded through the streets in honour of the Virgin. Elsewhere there are gastronomic festivals (*sagri*), when local delicacies come into season: at Alghero in January (sea urchins), in Muravera pre-Easter (citrus), and at Aritzo in October (chestnuts).

LEFT *Flowers and becostumed townsfolk aboard a carnival float for Sardinia's biggest 'sagra' which starts on 1 May and reaches a riotous climax on the night of 4 May*

Costa Smeralda

Sardinia is one of the top holiday spots for mainland Italians and nowhere on this island is there a more glamorous seaside paradise than the Smeralda Coast to the northeast. Legend has it that the narrow creeks and inlets of the coast here often provide refuge for sailors caught in storms in the Tyrrhenian reaches of the Mediterranean. But it remained a very neglected section of Sardinian coast until the 1960s, when a rather distinguished sailor dropped anchor here during a storm, saw its amazing beauty when the skies cleared and decided to turn it into one of the glitziest resorts in the Mediterranean. That sailor, the story goes, was Prince Karim Aga Khan, world leader of the Ismaili Muslims, and known as the millionaire playboy prince. Much of the story may be apocryphal, but the truth is that the Aga Khana *did* form a consortium which transformed the Emerald Coast into what it is today.

The main town of Porto Cervo has a village feel about it and this is where the tourist incomers rub shoulders with the affluent residents and villa homeowners. The area is an interesting mixture of scenery and style, with smart yachts and Moorish villas contrasting with a rugged coast and its mountainous backdrop. Every year in September the Sardinia Cup sailing regatta is held off the coast, involving quite a few famous boats – and faces. It was here, remember, that Princess Diana stayed with Dodi al-Fayed when they were plagued by photographers immediately before flying to Paris in 1997. The rest of the tragic story, we now know, is history.

LEFT *The rugged coastline and the beautiful waters of the Tyrrhenian reaches of the Mediterranean on the dazzling Smeralda (Emerald) Coast in northeast Sardinia*

BELOW *The smart yachts and Moorish-style villas of residents or holiday-homers on part of the exclusive Smeralda resort developed in the 1960s by the Aga Khan*

Cagliari

Most travellers who see Cagliari for the first time would sympathize wholeheartedly with the English writer D H Lawrence, who described the Sardinian capital thus: 'It is strange and rather wonderful, not a bit like Italy.' In fact, this is true of a great deal of the island, but Cagliari may have had a special place in the writer's heart because it reminded him of Jerusalem. And Cagliari, whose name means simply 'Castle', is easy to take to. Situated in the centre of the narrow southern coast, the city has a central 'citadel' area of narrow streets, called Castello, that forms the old town which has its roots in Roman times when, even then, it was the capital.

Within the old town, there are churches aplenty and most of the sights are worth seeing. These include the cathedral and the famous Elephant Tower, plus one of the best possible views of the city. This is through the arch of the Bastione San Remy, which is a magnificent terrace reached by a flight of marble steps. The district known as Marina is somewhat like Castello with its narrow streets but is a great deal busier with people shopping and going about their business.

And near the shuttered windows and balconies of the Villanova district there is the 5th-century Basilica di San Saturnino, which is one of Sardinia's oldest churches.

For anyone suffering from city-fatigue, Cagliari has Poetto, a generous stretch of sandy beach quite close by. Besides which, the city is the ideal jumping-off point for exploring the island's entire southwest region, which has many good beaches, archaeological sites and a number Nuragic ruins. These are what remains of the mysterious pre-historic race that came to the island around 1500BC and established about 30,000 circular, fortified structures, of which about 7000 still exist. One of the best examples is a village near Pula to the south, which has the remains of an amphitheatre, forum, baths, temple and kasbah. Like mainland Italy, Sardinia takes us deeper into the past.

BELOW *The arch on the terrace of the Bastione San Remy offers splendid views of the city. It is reached by a flight of marble steps from the Passeggiata Copert in Castello*

ABOVE *Washing strung across the balconies of a house in Cagliari's Villanova district, which is home to one of the island's oldest churches*

LEFT *Cagliari's Marina district is livelier than Castello with plenty of shops, businesses and restaurants – plus a handful of historic remains which are worth a visit*

Index

Acknowledgements

The Automobile Association wishes to thank the following photographers and organizations for their assistance in the preparation of this book.

Abbreviations for the picture credits are as follows – (t) top; (b) bottom; (l) left; (r) right; (c) centre; (dps) double page spread; (AA) AA World Travel Library

1 AA/Clive Sawyer; 2-3 AA/Simon McBride; 4-5 AA/Simon McBride; 8-9 AA/Jim Holmes; 10-11b AA/Alex Kouprianoff; 11t AA/Peter Wilson; 12tl AA/Simon McBride; 12-13 AA/ Alex Kouprianoff; 14 AA/Simon McBride; 15cr AA/Dario Miterdiri; 15b AA/Clive Sawyer; 16t AA/Simon McBride; 16bl AA/Peter Wilson; 17 AA/Simon McBride; 18 AA/Simon McBride; 19 AA/Simon McBride; 20-21 AA/Tony Souter; 22 AA/Tony Souter; 23tl AA/Tony Souter; 23cr AA/Tony Souter; 23b AA/Tony Souter; 24 Pictures Colour Library; 25 LOOK Die Bildagentur der Fotografen GmbH/Alamy; 26-27 Dan Santillo/Alamy; 28-29 AA/Tony Souter; 30 SIME/Gusso Luca/4Corners; 31 Gary Cook/Alamy; 32-33 SIME/Ripani Massimo/4Corners; 33br SIME/Kaos03/4Corners; 34-35 AA/ Max Jourdan; 36t AA/Max Jourdan; 36b AA/Max Jourdan; 37 AA/Max Jourdan; 38tl SIME/Dutton Colin/4Corners; 38-39 AA/Clive Sawyer; 40t AA/Anna Mockford & Nick Bonetti; 40bl AA/Clive Sawyer; 41 AA/Max Jourdan; 42-43b AA/Anna Mockford & Nick Bonetti; 43t AA/Anna Mockford & Nick Bonetti; 44-45 AA/Max Jourdan; 45tr AA/Max Jourdan; 46-47 AA/Simon McBride; 48 AA/Clive Sawyer; 49 AA/Clive Sawyer; 50tl AA/Anna Mockford & Nick Bonetti; 50 AA/ Anna Mockford & Nick Bonetti; 51 AA/Anna Mockford & Nick Bonetti; 52 AA/Anna Mockford & Nick Bonetti; 53l AA/Anna Mockford & Nick Bonetti; 53r AA/Simon McBride; 54-55 AA/Anna Mockford & Nick Bonetti; 56l AA/Anna Mockford & Nick Bonetti; 56-57 AA/Anna Mockford & Nick Bonetti; 58-59 AA/Anna Mockford & Nick Bonetti; 60-61 SIME/Angeli Nicola /4Corners; 62 AA/Anna Mockford & Nick Bonetti; 63tr AA/Pete Bennett; 63b AA/Anna Mockford & Nick Bonetti; 64 4Corners/Cozzi Guido; 65 SIME/Baviera Guido/4Corners; 66cl AA/Anna Mockford & Nick Bonetti; 66 AA/Max Jourdan; 67t AA/Anna Mockford & Nick Bonetti; 67b AA/Anna Mockford & Nick Bonetti; 68-69 Charles Bowman Phot212/axiomphotographic.com; 70-71 AA/Simon McBride; 72 AA/Simon McBride; 73 AA/Simon McBride; 73tr AA/Simon McBride; 73cr AA/Simon McBride; 74 AA/ Simon McBride; 75tr AA; 75b AA/Simon McBride; 76cl AA/ Simon McBride; 76bl AA/Simon McBride; 76cr AA/Clive Sawyer; 77 AA/Simon McBride; 78 AA/Terry Harris; 79tr AA/Ken Paterson; 79b AA/Clive Sawyer; 80t AA/Terry Harris; 80bl AA/Clive Sawyer; 81 AA/Ken Paterson; 82 AA/ Terry Harris; 83 AA/Terry Harris; 83tr AA/Terry Harris; 84-85 AA/Ken Paterson; 86 AA/Ken Paterson; 87t AA/Ken Paterson; 87bl AA/Ken Paterson; 87br AA/Ken Paterson; 88 AA/Terry Harris; 89bl AA/Terry Harris; 89r AA/Terry Harris; 90-91 AA/Terry Harris; 92-93b AA/Tony Souter; 93t AA/ Tony Souter; 94tl AA/Terry Harris; 94-95 AA/Terry Harris; 96 AA/Terry Harris; 97tl AA/Ken Paterson; 97r AA/Ken Paterson; 98-99 AA/Terry Harris; 99br AA/Ken Paterson; 100 AA/Terry Harris; 101 AA/Terry Harris; 101tr AA/Terry Harris; 102bl AA/Terry Harris; 102-103 AA/Terry Harris; 103r AA/Terry Harris; 104-105 AA/Simon McBride; 106 AA/ Tony Souter; 107t AA/Tony Souter; 107b SIME/Nagy Zoltan/ 4Corners; 108-109 AA/Clive Sawyer; 109br AA/Clive Sawyer; 110 AA/Simon McBride; 111 AA/Simon McBride; 112 AA/ Simon McBride; 113 AA/Simon McBride; 114tl AA/Clive Sawyer; 114b AA/Clive Sawyer; 115 Richard Osbourne/Blue Pearl Photographic/Alamy; 116tl AA/Clive Sawyer; 116-117 AA/Clive Sawyer; 117tr Maurizio Valentini/NHPA; 118-119 AA/Max Jourdan; 120-121 AA/Clive Sawyer; 121br AA/Max Jourdan; 122t AA/Max Jourdan; 122b AA/Max Jourdan; 123tr AA/Max Jourdan; 123b AA/Max Jourdan; 124bl SIME/ Giovanni Simeone/4Corners; 125 SIME/Giovanni Simeone/ 4Corners; 126 AA/Max Jourdan; 127 AA/Max Jourdan; 128-129 AA/Tony Souter; 129tr AA/Tony Souter; 130 AA/Max Jourdan; 131 AA/Max Jourdan; 132-133 SIME/Johanna Huber/4Corners; 134 SIME/Johanna Huber/4Corners; 135 SIME/Johanna Huber/4Corners; 136-137 AA/Clive Sawyer; 138 AA/Clive Sawyer; 139 SIME/Baviera Guido/4Corners; 140-141 SIME/Johanna Huber/4Corners; 142-143 SIME/ Johanna Huber/4Corners; 144-145 AA/Neil Setchfield; 146tl AA/Neil Setchfield; 146 AA/Neil Setchfield; 147 AA/Neil Setchfield; 148 AA/Clive Sawyer; 149 AA/Neil Setchfield; 149tr AA/Clive Sawyer; 150bl AA/Clive Sawyer; 150-151 AA/ Clive Sawyer; 152tl AA/Neil Setchfield; 152cl AA/Neil Setchfield; 152 AA/Neil Setchfield; 153 AA/Neil Setchfield; 154-155 AA/Neil Setchfield; 155br AA/Neil Setchfield; 156 AA/Neil Setchfield; 157 AA/Neil Setchfield; 157tr AA/Neil Setchfield.

GATEFOLDS
Treasures of Amalfi: Gatefold: Amalfi town, SIME/Giovanni Simeone/4Corners Images. DPS opener: Cathedral in Amalfi, SIME/Baviera Guido/4Corners Images. Lemons for sale, AA/ Max Jourdan. Ceramics, Vietri sul Mare, SIME/Pignatelli Massimo/4Corners

Ponte Vecchio, Florence: Gatefold, Ponte Vecchio, AA/Simon McBride. DPS opener, Ponte Vecchio at sunset, AA/Clive Sawyer. Detail of Ponte Vecchio, AA/Clive Sawyer. Jewellery shops, M.Flynn/Alamy

Food & Markets, Rome: Gatefold, Campo dei Fiori Market, AA/Clive Sawyer. DPS opener, Cheese and meats at Volpetti on Via Marmorata, AA/Clive Sawyer. Ice cream cones, AA/ Clive Sawyer. Bread at Volpetti on Via Marmorata, AA/Clive Sawyer. Daffodils, Campo dei Fiori Market, AA/Clive Sawyer

Carnevale, Venice: Gatefold, Venice Carnival, Bruno Morandi/ Robert Harding/Photolibrary. DPS Opener, Rialto Bridge, Images Etc Ltd/Alamy. Full page, gilded theatre mask, AA/ Clive Sawyer. Venice Carnival, Gimmi/Cuboimages. Procession, Venice Carnival, AA/Dario Miterdiri

Every effort has been made to trace the copyright holders, and we apologize in advance for any unintentional omissions or errors. We would be pleased to apply any corrections in any following edition of this publication.